Domestication

Published by McWest & Associates
ISBN: 978-1-971928-24-1

Domestication

Domesticity in Relation to Social Psyche & Identity

Baruch Menache

SECTION I: FOUNDATIONS & DEFINITIONS

I.1 DOMESTICATION AND THE POTENTIAL OF SOCIETY

AUTHOR'S NOTATION: We are broaching the subject of domestication, yet the reader should interpret the term as a kind of fashionable construct, such as "domesticated life," so that we do not view it in political terms, like "public vs. private life," but rather in the sense of domestication as it appears in the psychological process and philosophical domain. We are seeking the intellectual framework of what it means not only as a term of usage but as a fundamental concept, and therefore the associations with its more political or social usage should be dismissed. The definition will not be introduced outright because the entire project is dedicated to the precise definition of domestication or the domesticated process.

One need not pay heed to the domestication process, even as it is substantial to a psychological endeavor, and without it, the provision would cause disruption to societal and individual systems. Instead, one can participate in the public sphere without domestic security, in which one can gain the complete and utter embodiment of public rumination, all without the deterrence of domesticating processes. This does not mean that domestication is somehow not an aspect of their being, but is overlooked or entirely circumvented, as a result, one participates wholeheartedly in the potential of society.

Saying domestication is 'overlooked' implies it does not exist in the psyche; in reality, the opposite is true. The public rumination, or the experience Pof participating in civilization, is the core of the domestication process and will always vanish in preference to its helm. The domesticated substance, that of validation to its parts (relatability to experienced personhood), must always be seen as elements of a directive that is taken from a public sphere. To what domesticated measure can one rely long after that participation takes effect, if it is only for the objective to serve as a conduit of the dissemination of its elements? More so, how can another public sentiment and that sentiment's domesticated process take charge when a novel interaction of that sentiment is in full swing?

We use the term 'potential' because it captures the role of chance and process in one's psychological journey. For why need the overindulgence of the societal realm if it were not for an individual process that would be advantageous for that task? The only advantage to such embodiment is the potential of society, where one is dedicated to a particular realm but, more importantly, to its potential.

Potential is a substance that must be endured within a system, without distraction from biological needs or desires. If one were to focus on biological needs, they could not fully engage with society's potential. If they had engaged in their biological needs and experiences, they would not have been able to participate in a way that allows one to follow its premise and potential comprehensively. At most, they would extend to an already permeating potential, partaking just enough to proclaim endurance, while covertly waiting for the moment of availability for biological input and thus, escape.

Many a time, we find a certain disheartenment with such a process, as if the one devoid of domestication is somehow lacking being itself. Among other things, we highlight the absence of domestication; whose very existence, devoid of a homebound or domesticated appearance, stirs a ripple of suspicion. Yet, we tend to cast less doubt on those deeply immersed in domestication who, nonetheless, remain disconnected from or disengaged with the realities of the public sphere, a disconnection that can be just as, if not more, profound in its sense of alienation. Instead, we are not to deliberate a process of balance between the two, for the genuine potential of an individual or social process is only available to the one who fully commits themselves to a particular system, devoid of domesticated demands, at least not existentially. Thereby, the utopian vision of correlating both under the umbrella of the proper formation of life is altogether an illusion. We care only about what constitutes a complete experience. If that complete experience requires balancing the two realms, we would be in a third context that allows no uninhibited participation.

I.2 Levels & Dynamics of Domestication

Domestication can occur at various levels, and its progression is symbiotic. The most fundamental level is personal domestication, as no form of domestication is more profound than this. Next comes social domestication, often associated with the family unit, where bonds are mutual and validating. Following this is structural domestication, which mirrors the relationship between suburbs and urban centers or the interconnected locales within city streets. Finally, there is political domestication, which refers to the assimilation of external cultures into a state's jurisdiction. These levels form the basic structure of domestication.

Domestication, in this context, represents the neutral and the natural interweaving of psychological elements that do not require a direct representation or centralized form of communication. The family unit serves as the most relatable example, especially when there is no external interference. Family members communicate in ways that allow for dynamic inferences without a specific goal or directive. The only separation occurs through the interplay between family members, such as the oldest and youngest child. This dynamic also applies to personal domestication, where thoughts transpire in a flowing conversation-like pattern, reflecting each another without external demands. Therefore, domestication always involves a degree of concentration and awareness, as reflection is inherent to its process.

For instance, the oldest child embodies the role of the eldest, while the youngest embodies their role. This pattern is learned from consciousness itself and applied within this context. What makes domestication unique is that it requires minimal representation, often neglecting representation in favor of familiarity. A dysfunctional family dynamic can emerge when representation becomes excessively differentiated, causing family members to prioritize similarity over dynamic inferences. In the case of the oldest and youngest, they might communicate not according to their roles but based on perceived similarities, which can reduce their conversation as hollow: merely a reflection of each other.

This mirrors the experience of someone caught in self-pity for days or weeks, without any alteration in the modality of internal domestication. The same few thoughts keep reaffirming each other in a cyclical pattern, without variation. It's as if the individual has detached from representation, allowing just enough space for thoughts to emerge, but not enough for any deviation from the mirror-like validation of those thoughts. If we were to transcribe the thoughts of someone trapped in self-pity, we would find a few basic patterns that repeat themselves, without any variation. That is, until the psyche enters into a new form of representation that sparks dynamic inferences, advancing the conversation.

Family units can operate in a similar way, providing validation that keeps the family bonded together. However, when there is no significant movement across time, this cannot be considered domestication, but rather a repetitive cycle of thoughts voiced by different family members.

The Dispersal and Preservation of Peak Consciousness

There are two psychological forms of domestication when discussing the process of distributing conscious substance throughout the psyche, such that it is considered dispersed and does not reawaken as a peak semblance of consciousness. Peak semblance is defined as the all-inclusive state in which consciousness is first introduced, while non-peak refers to a state where one cannot return to the original condition due to a process of distillation.

It is possible to retain peak semblance for an extended period, as long as no process intervenes to alter or encapsulate it. Though distinct from simple memory capacity or perceptual acuity, peak semblance still persists and functions similarly to the initial state. However, once a further process of domestication takes place, through methods to be discussed, the substance loses its vitality, wholeness, embodiment, and the full range of both benefits and deficiencies inherent in peak semblance.

Through mental discipline, it is possible to maintain peak semblance throughout an adult lifespan by establishing a framework that prevents the various forms of domestication from affecting it.

The first and most prominent form of domestication involves making consciousness available in preliminary layers and fortifying these layers during their dispersal, effectively settling them into the early stages of consciousness development. Another method involves overlaying a contextual layer onto the consciousness sentiment, separate from direct exposure to the breakdown of consciousness itself. This approach involves analyzing the content in detail without justly departing from the original notion of consciousness, much like traditional domestication. As long as we study conscious substance without allowing it to follow its natural progression into preliminary layers, it remains contained.

Wholesome vs. Partial Domestication

There are two perspectives for which we could perceive domestication as a social particular: wholesome and partial. Wholesome domestication refers to the experience of being shaped by one's environment in a way that is fully internalized and re-expressed as a recreated, autonomous self. Partial domestication, on the other hand, involves retaining thematic elements of earlier domestic experiences without achieving complete recreation or integration.

The trajectory of psychological development reveals that domestication begins as a natural process; shaping the individual from the start. This foundational domestication forms the person and provides a full representation of their reality. As such, the nurturing environment that gives rise to the sense of self is considered a form of natural domestication. Even if this process is fragmented, inconsistent, or dysfunctional, it does not negate the individual's development. Rather, as the individual absorbs and responds to their environment, they begin to form a coherent self. This initial phase concludes once the person reaches a stage of autonomy; when they start to see themselves as the primary agent within their own experience.

At this point, the individual transitions from being a recipient of domestication to becoming its source. However, a discrepancy arises between the internalized self as a domesticated force and the external influences that originally shaped them. To achieve wholesome domestication, the individual must reconcile this fissure, integrating both original context and current autonomy.

For example, as individuals enter stages of social development, they form friendships. These early relationships can be seen as partial domestications; initial expressions of autonomy fashioned by personal initiative. Even so, the influences of their earlier environment remain present, subtly affecting these relationships. While the individual begins to exert more agency, they are not yet fully autonomous; thus, wholesome domestication is not necessary or achievable. These relationships serve as transitional steps toward self-definition.

As childhood continues, these partial domestications, such as friendships; would deepen. These evolving connections provide space for the individual to express and refine their own domesticated force, rather than being passively shaped by their surroundings. This maturation occurs through more profound social bonds and, eventually, intimate relationships. In such contexts, the individual seeks not dependency but autonomy; actively determining the environment rather than being formed by it. They become the domesticating force within their social context.

The family unit, in this framework, functions as a domestic structure that validates and affirms the individual's developing force. It supports their transition into wholesome domestication by offering a social environment in which the individual's internal autonomy can manifest outwardly. Though wholesome domestication relies on social interaction and environmental structures, it is ultimately rooted in the individual, who becomes its motivating force, even as these structures remain interactive and responsive to them.

Still, domestication is inherently relational. It cannot occur in total isolation. Wholesome domestication is preserved when an individual incorporates and embodies the environmental elements that formed them; retrieving and expressing these in themselves and in the thematic social context they create alongside others. This balance between self and environment sustains the authenticity of the domesticated self.

In contrast, partial domestication involves selectively recreating fragments of one's original environment. Rather than passively receiving influence, the individual actively reinterprets and revitalizes these elements to maintain their psychological relevance; without being wholly dependent on them. The objective is to surround oneself with a structured environment that reflects and draws out the vitality of one's conscious development. This serves as a living reminder of one's origins, sustaining an inner world that remains fertile for growth, reflection, and emulation.

I.3 Trauma & Consciousness Storage

Early on, in the case of individual psychological processes, domestication would be considered the interactivity of experience; think melancholic states or high interactive modalities, in which the interactivity, which is psyche fragments participating with one another to validate each other, would then have the disillusionment of peak consciousness that remains as a separate entity of the psyche.

Although if you consider consciousness as direct experience, it cannot be the case of being direct or indirect; it is stored as a memory, which, if retracted in a certain fashion, would be viewed (at least in psyche terms) as an experience of consciousness itself. In the general case, consciousness is stored in a partition of psyche processes that is directed away from individuation.

Thus, we have the traumatic instance, which is a storage of consciousness sentiment that does not delineate or deviate in time, but rather is entrenched in place, almost as if it has not changed from its commencement. The reason for this is that it is stored not by virtue of its traumatic endeavor (which is, according to Freud, a repressed arena of the psyche), but rather it is in the recess of the psyche, which contains conscious material; and trauma is always associated with consciousness.

If retracted from that memory base, and done so in a coherent manner, one will receive the psyche elements of consciousness as if it were a true and direct experience of consciousness, despite the fact that the perceptual experience of such is antiquated. In short, to evaluate why this circumstance is true or how it is possible, we need not look further than the perceptual mode itself. Because perceptual systems are an aggregation of external formations, and consciousness is substance that cannot be individuated, perceptual reception of said process does not work in a coherent manner; and thus one is exposed to consciousness without the mediation of perceptual modality.

Noticeably, there is a certain circuit of perception, for if not, the information would not be experienced; but it is a small process compared to the complex nature of perceptual reception. Because of this, the storage of consciousness material is, in fact, direct experience in perpetual motion; almost like a sustaining a computer bug in one's head that goes in cyclical form without time and space.

Perceptual modality affords consciousness per time and space. However, when perception deviates from this modality, there is no time or space. Instead, consciousness experiences itself as if it were encountering time and space for the first time. This state is its most fundamental mental sense, unrestricted from distinctions of first or last, and thus outside the typical dimensions of regular psyche behavior. It is akin to what physics might describe as the "fifth dimension."

This is why the concept of memory can dilute understanding. Memory, as commonly represented in our models (such as in computers), implies something stored away that does not necessarily connect back to living systems. In this case, however, it is not memory per se, but the true experience of consciousness in its original, unique format. Memory may serve as the axis laterally of this experience, but it need not be categorized as such.

For instance, it is possible to be momentarily drawn back to an early consciousness experience simply by encountering a smell or a sight. Freud suggests that associations bring repressed material back into consciousness, but we could also dictate that these initiates provide an entry point into a modality of that prior consciousness, buried deep within the mind. In this case, the experience is highlighted without the typical "track record" of memory lineage.

Although associations might seem to form a kind of memory lineage; each image or association reflecting another until it reaches the source material; it would not be accurate to consider them a pathway for memory. There is no external context to facilitate the processing of such a lineage.

For comparison, consider the concept of generational lineage. One cannot attach to their ancestral lineage unless they are within the context of familial systems. A person does not typically think of their lineage unless it is tied to their adherence to family or its concepts. Similarly, associations do not lead back to lineage concepts, nor does a person necessarily have any experience of lineage throughout their life, even though many associations might have brought such concepts to the surface. The connection occurs only within the context that houses that direction of memory.

When considering memory itself, if one is tasked with recalling a childhood experience, the first step would be to establish a context for "childhood" as a whole; almost as if it were a specific realm. If someone has not constructed such a framework, they would be confused by the request and be unable to provide a coherent reaction. This is because they lack the context needed to access that memory; without it, there is no entry point.

If the process were simply based on associations, we could theoretically retrieve that memory. However, we are venturing into areas less defined by differentiation. Certain childhood memories are indeed conscious experiences, and it's possible to access them through association. But we could also argue that only non-conscious or subconscious material can be accessed through the proper channels of memory. They will be emanating from an individual who presumes the happenstances of their domestication as if their social-public is concerned with those very ideas and consequently, a reality. They will even venture the premise that, even as the public does not espouse those ideas for which they are determined to domestication, they should be following them because of their importance in some way.

"They should be engaging in this period of history or this historical figure because there is something true and real within it." Nevertheless, such argumentation can be made for any important element that might be overlooked by public discourse. Their concluding theories will be based on that. Only with the complete separation from that domestic reality will the individual be able to enjoin in the procedure of potential that accurately mirrors the societal process. This is something the individual eventually embodies.

In some ways, domestication is the need for more justification, for it is the neglect of reality in its most augmented form. To follow potential should be the natural causation of individuals, although what is natural is not always successful.

For example, evolutionary spirit has the natural inclination to follow a reality framework in which the most dominant creature becomes the most successful. Yet, the result of evolution is contrary to this, as domesticated elements have proven to be paramount traits for survival. The dinosaur did not outlive its counterparts simply by sheer size, but rather due to its homebody elements, which protected it from extinction events, a trait that many birds, its descendants, still carry.

Whatever we may say about the future of animal life, we can be certain that the last on that list will be the dog and the cat, for they are domesticated by the dominant life form. As long as they remain domesticated, and higher life form thrives, they will remain part of the survival chain.

Despite all this, domestication represents a deviation from nature, and therefore, it becomes essential for individuals to engage with this process. The inclusion or exclusion of a domesticated entity only makes sense within the context of extracting potential from an individual's unique form of potential. While there is a form of potential within the domesticated group, it is not internalized in the same way; it's not meant to be extracted but is only reflected upon when needed by the public sphere. Similar to an advertisement, which sometimes serves to represent something for the public, and at other times, is merely an establishment's attempt at participation.

However, within the individual's parameters, their domesticated quality can have significance for direct extraction; entering into the cave, interacting with material in a free modality, and returning with a vantage of insight that is purposeful because of its domestication. When domestication follows its correct route, it formulates the package for extraction, which will always benefit the public realm, simply because it follows the interaction process to formulate its inherent outlook for later consumption.

Without the potential to manifest, the entire chain of reactions that leads back to domestication becomes lost. The current era of domestication represents not just a stage in human development, but the materialization of historical potential, a set of latent possibilities and tendencies; that have now been fully integrated into the structures and processes of domestication itself. If we remove the foundation of this potential, domestication will lose its traction from footing which espouses against that climate and will revert to a more primitive form of domestication.

Natural domestication is based on a bond that involves a certain agreement. The rules and parameters of this relationship are based on the potential that has been reached. When that potential no longer progresses, the permeation of those elements becomes lost to the homebody, and the agreement loses its sophisticated basis. The relationship body will then follow an outdated version of itself, which reflects the current status of external potential. Typically, the domesticated body will not participate properly with the current potential but will instead rely on an earlier, more articulated version of that potential.

For example, if the full potential of understanding has reached the realization that relationship bonds are complex psychological processes; and that there is a psychological history shaping the bond, both as a shared experience and as individual selves; then even an unarticulated version of this understanding can still be perceived. It would replay the dynamic of the relationship, guided by this complex, internalized information. Where significant defects exist in the relational body, one endures a form of domestication; one that becomes a dynamic within the history of psychoanalysis. This arises from the unarticulated form, where a proper procedure of domestication would involve recognizing the psychological process within the flow of sociality, and then, extending outward, into society itself.

We can even claim that, so long as society's potential appears to follow a path of progress, the domesticated realm acts as the point of reflection; where the unarticulated form of that potential quietly resides. A general rule can be observed: in periods of progress, the point of reflection is domestication; in periods of stagnation or regression, it is the realm of potential that demands the most attention.

It may be difficult for potentiality to lead without a domesticated inference; for what, then, halts progress that advances too far ahead, or worse, applies a form of progress that, by its very nature, can never be domesticated?

Trauma & Fragmentation

Domestication differs from that of the corporeal entity, as it involves an interaction with the conscious substrate without securing a particular domain, distinct and generalized under its own constitution. Domestication does not follow a constitution or a conceptual framework since it is not inherently conceptual; rather, it is the socialized material of consciousness substance. It is distinct from consciousness per se because it is embodied in a social element and partialized in a fragmented sense. As such, it does not fulfill the role or comprehensiveness of consciousness itself.

These two elements are the criteria by which domestication is distinct from consciousness, but not necessarily distinct from the corporeal entity; this is an entirely different matter related to non-conscious realms. The first of these criteria is that domestication is socialized, whereas encapsulation of consciousness is not. Consciousness is a substrate of intellectual data that lies beyond the contained framework of intellectuality. Domestication, however, is the socialized element. This means that it is specifically the intellectual material that can be embodied as a socialized exhibition, such that all the remnants of consciousness that cannot be socialized fall by the wayside and are not explored as subjects within the realm of socialization.

We have often observed that there are consciousness sentiments that cannot be socialized. For example, mathematical formulas and their inherent philosophical theories do not lack social ability because they are more abstract than regular socialized content, but because they enter a domain of thought that has not breached the realm of sociality, though this may change depending on the development of confident domestication. It is instead a matter of what can be socialized in the real environment. Domestication is highly dependent on environmental factors. It cannot simply domesticate, or participate in a sociality of encapsulated consciousness, if the environment is not in alignment, and there is no exchange relevant to that material.

It is comparable to a scholar of an ancient civilization whose knowledge has no effect on the bearing of existing socialization, despite the fact that it may very well be socialable. Because there is no exchange for such remnants, it remains a consciousness substrate that does not have a domesticated counterpart.

Besides the regular conversation about domestication as a mediation of representational models with a global mapping aligned with the full scope of Consciousness, domestication has an alternative effect. When domestication is followed thoroughly, and in contrast to something representational or interactive for that matter, one enjoys the experience of being fully scoped to an analysis that is beyond the parameters of structural regiments or contextual overlays. This becomes possible when there is the ability to be extraterrestrial throughout the scope of the psyche in all its pockets. Domestication does not follow its regular method of traversing, but rather enters into a sphere where it is as if one is downloading the psyche into a database. In this mode, it is not working off the psychic process itself but rather as a mirror, attempting to extract data without being fully embodied in the presence of the movement of the psyche.

In this way, we have come to view domestication as pertaining to family-body values, for they are naturally socialized elements. But in reality, domestication is anything that may be socialized in the current forum. It just so happens that, in this epoch, the family-body has served as socialized material, while in some sense serving as a foundational element of human progression; accordingly, they work hand in hand.

Socialization is the familiar data afforded to the process of human experience onto itself, such that it becomes specific to individualization. Thus, we construct the entire form of domestication around what is familiar to the individual; this being distinct from consciousness itself, so that domestication is limited in what it can attach within consciousness, whereas consciousness is broad and can extend into many arenas, as long as it adheres to the laws of nature, or, in this case, the laws of consciousness.

Domestication follows a specific regulation: it requires criteria that are socialized aspects, yet also fragmented from consciousness. This allows it to fulfill its role in a dynamic process that brings familiarity. What becomes familiar must balance between what is less familiar and what is more familiar, creating a dynamic nature that allows domestication to thrive. In the end, domestication requires this fragmentation of consciousness to fulfill the roles each participant embodies, one becoming more familiar, the other distributing that familiarity.

The material through which domestication begins is real-time consciousness data. This contrasts with the corporeal entity, which operates according to a far-reaching memory, as long as that memory connects to current sociality. Even the corporeal entity cannot fully access antiquated consciousness, as it remains tethered to the present social context. It engages with memory that spans back in time, nevertheless domestication cannot function within outdated history. It must instead be driven by current consciousness data and the sociality that emerges from it.

Even if domestication did not occur in prior consciousness, a situation that is quite common, it cannot be domesticated in the present if it has not been part of an ongoing experience of consciousness; it lacks the sociality needed to become familiar. The psyche does not need all forms of consciousness to be domesticated, only those exposed to it through the psyche and sociality. These are the derivatives of current consciousness experiences. Thus, sociality arises from the overexposure to consciousness, or more specifically, the experience of being exposed to consciousness; through which domestication becomes necessary to provide the sociality required to fragment these experiences.

Domestication, therefore, is something that comes into play only after the experience of consciousness. It is not a conceptual construct or an idea in formation; it's a tool that emerges in the aftermath of that experience. Of course, domestication can help preclude exposure to early forms of consciousness, much like the corporeal entity, but it can only do so as an addition to the ongoing need for domestication.

For example, one might domesticate based on the historical precedents of their lineage, not because they were directly exposed to their ancestors' experiences, but because they apply that memory in conjunction with current experiences to facilitate the domestication process. Sociality does not concern itself with how consciousness was originally formed; it's only concerned with the fact that it's now necessary to fragment those elements. Memory traces can aid the process, but the focus remains on the socialized effect; domestication of exposure, rather than anything else.

The domestication of consciousness does not rely on a specific material lineage but follows an indirect relationship. If one is exposed to content in a particular domain of consciousness, they must domesticate it, as long as there is a container through which that experience is processed. Once contained, the individual may proceed as they see fit. This is similar to two friends in a city, whose interactions are shaped by the surrounding conscious experiences, yet they hold content of an arbitrary nature, not necessarily linked to the original experiences. Still, this is sufficient to allow the domestication of their interactions in a social context. The exposure itself drives the experience.

However, there is a caveat: there must be an indirect relationship between the consciousness material and sociality. When that relationship deviates, sociality can continue, but without fragmenting or diluting consciousness, since the conversation no longer engages the subject. Without this link, deviation leads to greater dilution.

The fastest form of domestication happens when sociality is rooted in content directly tied to the original exposure. In this case, sociality reflects parts of the full experience. The slowest form occurs when the deviation is so large that only the exposure itself remains. At this point, the original material is no longer considered or followed; instead, new content emerges, but with only a distant connection to the original exposure. With this level of indirectness, dilution takes longer, and domestication may take months, years, or even a lifetime to fully unfold from a single exposure.

When there is adherence to domestication, even as consciousness demands the reciprocation of representational value, it becomes a shadow of that very consciousness. It no longer remains truly domesticated, as that is not its inherent structure. Instead, it becomes reluctant to participate fully in consciousness and, in doing so, transforms into its shadow. Any interaction that persists despite the presence of consciousness should be regarded as a shadow of consciousness. Its reality is activated by consciousness, and it can only maintain its coherence as domestication by following the missing aspects of consciousness, its lack of self-validation and its need for interactivity.

It's as though this interactivity can persist and take root even within consciousness as the surrounding environment because it derives its form from the very absence of that element within consciousness. In this way, it inevitably becomes a shadow of consciousness.

I.4 SIMULATED CONVERGENCE

Every society has the tendency to simulate the convergence of interactive aspects into the already established and infrastructural system of consciousness rumination, rather than unaffectedly allocating it. The convergence is engineered to offer capabilities that, when genuine convergence occurs, can entertain the real material required for both sides of the equation.

Typically, this convergence is mistaken for genuine, as both elements, industrial and consciousness; appear to be in direct alignment. However, because of the very real separation from genuine exposure, this locale has the ability to experience convergence in their privacy without adhering to the complete engagement of rumination.

This becomes evident in the lack of dynamic exchange between society and its processes. Although industrialized aspects are in use, they are essentially recreations of those processes, not actual engagements with them.

Positive Deviance & Limits

Petrou et al. (2018) made the case, stating: "To the best of our knowledge, this is the first empirical field validation of an effect that had previously only been addressed in the laboratory... confirmed among employees reporting on their real-life creative performance at work, as perceived by themselves and their coworkers. This phenomenon falls under the overarching term of positive deviance, where employees break rules to facilitate work goals rather than to harm the organization." (Petrou et al., 2018)."

And further premised that it is only the case of more potential when, in fact, there was a traditional and organizational structure that was previously adhered to. This is the task of being fully immersed into a system of whatever their ambition, and to then defy those parameters; not to depart or to 'harm the organization,' but to follow a more thoroughly in-line creative ideation of itself; to extract the potential.

As Petrou notes: "Interestingly, though, the results did not only provide support for the hypothesized effect but also revealed an additional condition under which rule-breaking relates (although less strongly) to creativity: namely, when problem-solving demands are low and organizational demands are also low… One possible explanation is that this specific condition (i.e., no need but also no obstacles for creativity) represents a relatively passive job condition that allows rule-breakers to express themselves without really having to strive for anything" (Petrou et al., 2018).[1]

There is the possibility of an engagement with domestication beyond the fellowship of potential, where the process serves no other purpose other than to enforce a sentiment of demystification. This will manifest as the biological foundation of the individual, for the rudimentary state of domestication is the cradle of one's system, but it will ultimately corrupt any formation of potential.

To illustrate, we can predict that the long-term potential of evolutionary beings might lead to a bio-human alliance, with intellect and biology increasingly aligned. As Yuval Noah Harari suggests in *Sapiens*: "At the time of writing, the replacement of natural selection

---

[1] Petrou, A., Van der Linden, D., & Salcescu, M. (2018). The relationship between prosocial rule-breaking and creativity: Field evidence from the workplace. Journal of Applied Psychology, 103(2), 1–12.

by intelligent design could happen in any of three ways: through biological engineering, cyborg engineering (cyborgs are beings that combine organic and non-organic parts), or the engineering of inorganic life."[2]

This is despite the biological system, or what we call the self-referential system; is not inherently designed for such input or realignment. Evolution is concerned solely with the propagation and survival of its own kind, not with establishing dominion over nature's possibilities.

To follow this trajectory, one would have to disregard the domesticated elements, those expressions of evolutionary demands, like validating the system itself; in order to fortify the human structure as an entity that does not rely on singularity or the sanctity granted by its designation as an individual.

For instance, there is nothing intrinsic to the domestication process that accepts physical alterations prompted by intellectual inquiry and industry. Such changes are foreign to the system for that which domestication upholds. This is not to suggest that the potential of the social endeavor should avoid such procedures, they are inevitable.

Naturally, there would be an attempt to redefine the self-referential system, but this would require altering consciousness itself, which leads us into the realm of consciousness—a topic outside the current scope of study. As Harari notes, "Perhaps another small change would be enough to ignite a Second Cognitive Revolution,

---

[2] Yuval Noah Harari, Sapiens: A Brief History of Humankind (New York: Harper, 2015)

create a completely new type of consciousness, and transform Homo sapiens into something altogether different." (Harari, Sapiens)[3]

Once the potential is unleashed into the social sphere and actively engaged, it extends into the domesticated realm, causing the bio-human effort to become either domesticated or rejected as incompatible with societal norms. If deemed incompatible, this deviation of potential is seen as incapable of being tamed within the familiar, dynamic landscape of individuality. Until potential has been domesticated, it must be pursued by individuals who exist outside the domesticated spectrum, as it cannot accommodate or validate a perspective that, at present, remains outside of domestication and has no foreseeable path toward it.

At this historical juncture, the bio-human process has not yet undergone full domestication. Therefore, it can only engage those who follow potential, not those entrenched in domesticated concerns. The inevitable future will see certain aspects of this process domesticated, transitioning from potential to actualization within both social and domestic spheres.

The difference between the social and the domesticated is largely semantic. A truly social endeavor is, in essence, a domesticated process. Similarly, domestication is inherently a social experience. The distinction arises from how these processes deviate from their original context. Sociality typically involves peers, where significance is communicated through outward dialogue or social cues, whereas domestic forms of socialization are less outward. The biological makeup and intimate nature of these realms have already facilitated sociality without formal dialogue. One need only observe the awareness of an adopted child seeking out a lost parental figure, who instinctively looks to fill an existential void. There is no need for a

---

[3] Ibid.

continuing dialogue; sociality is already embedded in the biological system. Ideas and exchanges begin to form between the parental figure and the child, despite no direct knowledge of each other or their respective makeup. In genuine domestication, sociality is more deeply embedded into the system, which is why familial bodies do not require the dialogical exchange that regular social systems rely on.

Social systems, for that matter, and their genuine experience, are the exchange of relatability or the validation of psyche elements; essentially the congested information of domestication. While there is potential for sociality removed from domestication, this would not, in its truest sense, be called sociality, but rather context-based interaction, such as in work environments or religious contexts.

These do not perform the essential work that genuine domestication does, because the sociality involved is inherently outward, which does not allow for the permeation of the full spectrum of psyche parts. Of course, we could find the extreme possibility on either side: where familiar domestication is rather the other performing, so that it does not seem like a vacuum of validation, but rather a deviation; especially in scenarios of overwhelming context or neglectful processes. Likewise, we could find sociality that outperforms familial domestication, involving deep dynamical processes with engagements of true vulnerabilities. Although, at this point, the distinction between friends and intimate partners, at least in the emotional sphere, becomes questionable.

An attempt to balance domestication and public experience is itself an endeavor that is fundamentally impossible. For if there are inklings of domestication, there will be a retracement of that potential; at least in what is possible for the individual and society. Likewise, if there is a domesticated realm in which one reaches the precipice of potential, it will not be the elements that are fundamental for the individual, nor for society.

This is the case, shifting from general deviation to a hacking of the psyche system; and, ultimately, to the detriment of society as an orderly whole. This is the case where a domesticated process, whether it is social, familial, or psychological; would engender public experience without leaving the confines of that very domestication. Meaning that the relatability or experience of contents as its validating process coincides simultaneously with public experience. In its finality, one must attempt to experience consciousness in its domesticated form while still remaining attached to that very consciousness.

Although this may seem like a utopian ideal that remains possible in theoretical terms, it is the case that consciousness, or its substance; is not available for relatability, due to the fact that it has surpassed its composite as being individualized, and thus unrelatable in its raw state.

The attempt to achieve this process carries potential detriments, first and foremost the risk of manipulating the consciousness system. Instead of going through the work of participating in a dissemination process, one takes the path of least resistance by simply gaining conscious experience in its raw form to permeate the entirety of personhood, thereby enabling the full scope of a conscious enterprise. Although it seems simple enough, that of relegating consciousness throughout personhood; because of the various constraints, structurally, socially, and physiologically, we must consider them to perform at adequate output.

Secondly, in the case of familial domestication, the experience could overwhelm the private nature of that sphere. It could, in essence, use its most vulnerable elements, the capacity for relatability; to access higher consciousness, a process which individual family members may lack the means to process or exchange in a dynamic fashion. Beyond the psychological detriment for individuals, there is the risk that the familial body becomes exposed to high forms of consciousness, simply due to its vulnerability and attachment to the domesticated process; this contrasts with the separation of different existential modalities.

Generally, exposure to consciousness depends on one's contextual participation or association. But in the case of adherence to a domesticated entity, especially a familial one, it could be the case that, by merely participating in that, the input of a consciousness modality would have the proponents unwillingly participate in that experience.

This offers sympathy to the estrangement of stranger characters in heavily domesticated environments, for the very opportunity of receiving a volume of consciousness that would disrupt the entire function of the domestication. Although sympathy is offered as a manner to understand the importance of avoiding domesticated consciousness in its direct manifestation, it is still the case that all domestication must serve and recognize its subservience in the face of consciousness. By the composite nature of domestication, it is merely the repositioning of conscious sentiments in manners seen fit by the parameters of domestication.

For illustration, familial domestication has its set parameters on conscious sentiments relating to life cycles and developmental stages of growth. This is not the sole criterion of consciousness, but it does justice to the specific aspects that are maintained in a domesticated mode. Most sensitive of the familial body, then, would be conscious sentiments from the public in concern with these elements, for already they are required to listen to such a juxtaposition. One cannot ignore incoming conscious sentiments, as the domesticated compartment of the brain is already processing that information against the domesticated postulation. The only method is proceeding with the exposure; but after the fact, the hierarchy is put in place, and all domestication is found in disfavor of genuine conscious exposure.

We see such a representation in renowned familial bodies, where the public representation of their structure and system has the participants of that domesticated feature automatically retrofitted with that representational element. This is not the direct downloading of consciousness into domesticated parameters, but it is enough to cause contestation and disruption within the domesticated entity. Participants of that domesticated quality must adhere, for public representation is a fundamental reality in some sense; to the experience of that representation. Thus, they are demanded to either separate from that domesticated feature or stay the course of that domesticated entity and simultaneously accept representation.

In this case, it's the cause of psychological disruption and systemic disruption, where the domesticated quality, that of relatability to individuated parts; is also being represented in the public through that specific admiration. Thus, it either retracts or constructs that domesticated feature as a representation, leaving the individual physiologically and psychologically torn between the two.

The truth of the matter is that the domesticated feature has become more of a skeletal structure at this point; the representation itself is the true effect of psychological experience, with only remnants of domestication preserving their individuated form. In this process, merging transforms into an 'othering,' paving the way for an impending disruption in psychological direction.

I.5 Disruption Dynamics

The argument against the domestication of externalities is valid, as it risks undermining the very parameters that define domestication, potentially turning into an externality itself. If a private space, such as one's home, is opened to the public in a way that alters its fundamental structure, the original domestication is lost. What it once was will no longer exist. The same applies to domesticated spaces that attract public attention; when that attention fades, the space often transforms from a private realm into a public one.

However, the only way to truly disrupt a domestication is either through public acquisition of the private sphere or by accommodating the public in a structural sense. If the physical boundaries of a domesticated space are opened to public engagement, causing alterations to its original form, then disruption is likely. But if the boundaries remain fixed, with the space restricted to the internal realm of domestication, no external influence can alter its integrity. No amount of external material, thought, or information can disrupt a domestication once it's established.

While disruptions can occur when content or ideas interact with a domesticated system, it's important to understand that the disruption is not caused by the content itself. Instead, it's the way the content is received within the system that triggers a shift in dynamics. This shift may have been latent, unnoticed, or underdeveloped until the content serves as the catalyst. In other words, the disruption was always embedded within the dynamic, but the content brought it to the surface. For example, in relationships, such as divorce, a change in content (e.g., shifting thoughts, feelings, or behaviors) alters the dynamic, eventually leading to the relationship's conclusion.

If content triggers a disruptive dynamic, it's misleading to attribute the disruption solely to the content itself. Rather, we must recognize that political and cultural elements influencing domestication may appear to play a role in the disruption. However, this does not mean the political context is the direct cause of the breakdown. In reality, these political elements have not fully engaged in the necessary dynamic exchange. The disruption arises from this misalignment, ultimately leading to separation.

An overload of specific content can also hinder the natural development of a dynamic system. For instance, a domestication based on intimacy, particularly physical intimacy, may struggle when burdened with content related to this theme. Such a system may not be equipped to handle this influx, resulting in failure due to a reluctance to grow. However, because dynamic exchange is reciprocal, the excessive content might cause one participant to disengage, placating the other or redirecting the exchange to nullify its disruptive potential. For the overload to result in true disruption, both parties must remain engaged in the exchange. If one party disengages, the dynamic will sever, regardless of the other party's continued involvement.

This distinction is important when considering public conversation or sociality versus standard content that is not part of real-time public rumination. In the case of public sociality, there is no risk of information excess because it's already integrated into the broader political system. The domestication will fully engage with the dynamic.

While information is often interpreted subconsciously, the dynamic regulates the willingness to explore these deeper layers. In contrast, content discussed in past or future public discourse, or within other broadcasting, tends to stagnate domestication. This content is contextually refined and bound to the individual's contribution, making it secondary to the overall context of the exchange.

I.6 Activating Consciousness in Domestication

If after the fact we have a peak form of consciousness, we need to find in where such takes place in the realm of domestication and onward to consciousness. There are two primary ways an individual can access consciousness when severed from the rumination process. The first involves recreating consciousness, as though civilization has been reborn and the individual is the first to engage with its foundational building blocks. In this process, memory traces of consciousness emerge, despite the initial assumption that the necessary details to initiate such a creation would be unavailable. Through this memory process, these traces begin to recreate the experience, not merely as a recreation, but as a lived memory.

The second method involves participating in the memory of a previously experienced consciousness, allowing that memory to disseminate information within the domesticated context. However, this approach disrupts the integrity of domestication, as it positions the individual outside the process, relying on the memory of consciousness rather than fully engaging with the structure.

Having memory as a conduit to the domesticated locale, without it being a mere recreation; is a difficult feat. The very act of recalling memory invokes the inception of infiltration, which mirrors the experience in real-time. The only difference is the structural separation, whereas in the case of schizophrenics, who lose the structural seamlessness, they begin to display misinterpretations of memory traces and reality.

However, memory can become a recreation of consciousness when there is an associated structural element in which one unreservedly participates, adapting to circumvent the memory of consciousness as if it were a newly formulated circumstance. We observe this in rituals, which are structural realms involving physicality and systematic adaptations. The sole purpose of these rituals is to recreate a consciousness sentiment from a memory trace.

Certain types of recreation are purposeful, particularly when individuals participate in these rituals at the behest of a fully cognizant realm of consciousness. For them, especially for the infantile state of individuals; the ritual does not function as a recreation but as the inception of consciousness, with no memory of something larger than itself. It is this very lack of broader consciousness that makes the ritual a perfected space. It is not a recreation of anything but rather an endowment of consciousness in the first place.

Yet, immediately upon the encroachment of elements of broader consciousness, the realistic endeavor retracts from the memory traces that are more dominant and recreates itself in the subservient or dependent space of the ritualistic context. There is a certain paradox: the visionaries of a ritual cannot partake in it. For the very act of providing memory traces that assist in making the ritual a conduit of consciousness renders them unavailable due to the predominant consciousness lying outside such recreation.

This is one of the many reasons why realistic endeavors must always maintain a community and traditionalist sense. They cannot be dependent upon individuals and their transitory inspirations. The very act of creating a ritualistic environment is a recreation of a higher level of consciousness to a lower effect in this recreation. In the community or traditionalist environment, there is a social permeation of dynamics that leads the individual to participate in the ritual. The lower strata of the individual participate wholeheartedly, while the upper strata merely engage for appearance or for personal interaction within their own context. It is as though we need the ritual to occur within the social dynamic without any creation from individuals so that it "just happens" to arrive at one's doorstep, thereby not requiring any individualistic detriment but instead expanding each participant's consciousness.

The recreation process takes shape when there is primarily physical activity, a change of location or space, an irregular format, or other mechanisms that provide a physical pronouncement to create a structural environment and a habitat for consciousness permeation. Without physicality as a participant, one is lost in a structural environment that serves as a habitat for the memory trace, allowing consciousness to permeate and hover without ever being a recreation, but rather a visitation of memory.

We may wonder about the possibility of recreation from mere memory; whether a complete embodiment of memory can serve as a source of consciousness. As long as there is no structural adherence, consciousness will find no rest. However, we can find structural adherence without physicality, due to residence and movement that accrue adequate physicality to recreate consciousness anew.

One can draw from their memory trace all its provisions, thereby becoming emptied of consciousness permeation within their domesticated environment. In this case, it becomes the individual's responsibility to revisit their memory traces, identify their patterns, and allow permeation to arise anew. Embodiment, one that leads to recreation, can also occur in a seemingly conceptual setting.

SECTION II: SOCIALITY & RELATIONSHIPS

II.1 FOUNDATIONS OF DOMESTICATION

AUTHOR'S NOTATION:

1) Expanding/domesticating the self.

2) Social buffers & integration.

3) Relational extremes (codependency vs. domestication).

The Expansion of Domestication: Renunciation or Availability

Domestication, whether through external perception (a grouping that contains a degree of validation among its members based on a strong representation of their bond) or internal domestication (the psyche's realm that retains a parameter-based habitat simply validating the other through a requisite domesticated entity), represents the interactive locale of the psyche. This locale is built and secluded from regular movements, following the depth of information rather than its breadth.

In this case, the domesticated realm can become so removed from regular psychic movements that it no longer serves as a domain offering a degree of consciousness through its relational material. Therefore, one can relinquish that domain by tearing its seams, either by recognizing the elevated connection to the regular psyche or by revealing its domesticated depths.

For example, a small family does not experience a strong degree of domestication because they have not encountered external agents that provide dynamic availability of validation. However, that domesticated experience can be expanded either by renunciation into broader public realms or by becoming available to further validating elements that exist within them. This follows a natural conversation that does not require regular consciousness interference; rather, the references themselves become the recognition of a broader state, without revealing the vantage point of that broader state.

These are the two ways to expand domestication: either by renunciation or by the availability of nuance within that domestication. Both paths reach a broader spectrum. This prevents the seclusion that can have adverse effects.

The Social Framework of Domestication: Psyche, Consciousness, and Vitality

The domestication of consciousness is a process that organizes a system socially rather than individually, with its value rooted in this sociality. When an individual with domesticated consciousness is removed from the social framework that validates it, signs of degeneration appear. Any process of domestication reflects similar processes within consciousness because, at its core, it entails the domestication of experience itself. To fully understand the social framework of domestication we must identify the parallels between these processes to discern both their similarities and their differences.

While it is true that a departure from civilization leads to degeneration in an individual's consciousness, the nature of this degeneration differs in someone who retains a domesticated form of consciousness. They do not degenerate because of a loss of attachment to consciousness itself. Rather, domestication is not defined by attachment to its origins, but by its dependence on a social framework that sustains its vitality. Without sociality, domestication cannot exist, as socialization provides the necessary buffer against the loss of attachment.

If someone detaches from civilization (and from consciousness and other external sources of thought), they need a buffer to redistribute and revitalize their domesticated space. Without such attachment, the state ceases to be one of domestication and instead become a detachment from all rumination.

This pseudo-attachment acts as a structural buffer contained by both individuals and societies. On the individual level, this involves periodically reacquiring reflection, which remains accessible within domestication but must stay subconscious to prevent the space from being perceived as de-domesticated. When the psyche retains a part still attached to former encounters with exposure and enters a domesticated space, it may experience discomfort. This lingering attachment becomes a vulnerability; a shadow cast by domestication.

However, if the psyche becomes overly domesticated, meaning repressed parts no longer engage in outward rumination; domestication itself becomes detached. A buffer zone then forms in the psyche between two domains: one of encapsulation and the other of domestication. This space preserves continuity while maintaining distance from both sides.

II.2 Psychological Dynamics within Sociality

Interpersonal Integration and Codependency

The process of engaging with another person's persona; whether that of a family member, close friend, or public figure; can occur along a spectrum. At one end, we find codependency, where the individual becomes enmeshed with the other's identity that their sense of self is lost. At the other end, we encounter a phenomenon we refer to as "the domestication of consciousness."

In this process, one actively, or perhaps unwittingly incorporates elements of another's perceived essence into their psyche, despite maintaining an awareness of the boundaries of such integration; preserving a sense of selfhood even as it undergoes restructuring. This restructuring materializes primarily to have the environment more hospitable to the incoming persona.

Aspects of regular personhood that serve this goal remain intact, supported by sophisticated reasoning, while elements that do not contribute or threaten the process are adapted to the new consciousness, often by adjusting to its opposition. For example, if someone dislikes distinction but is engaging with a persona that embodies these traits, they may reframe their dislike as something absent in their new persona, rather than an inherent flaw. This awareness is safeguarded by what we call a "social buffer," an internal mechanism that prevents complete absorption and helps preserve the dynamic flow of the self.

Domesticating Relationships vs. Codependency

Codependency differs from domestication in that, in codependency, one becomes wholly enmeshed with the persona of the other, losing their sense of individuality. In contrast, in domesticated relationships, one integrates the perceived persona of the other within their psyche, but does not fully adopt another identity. The individual does not perceive themselves as interacting with a complete persona, but rather with a form of consciousness or an idealized embodiment that they recognize as potential consciousness within a specific environment.

This is often seen in the context of personages, but it could also apply to a spouse whom one venerates for an ideal or even a friendship where social connection is glorified. For example, an introvert; or someone who perceives sociality as the central sphere of existence; may become infatuated with the concept of sociality itself, leading them to adore simple relationships. Once glorified, they may believe that the relationships represent the full scope of consciousness and, in turn, domesticate that aspect.

Codependency is characterized by an unchecked merging where the boundaries of individuality dissolve. In contrast, the domestication of relationships involves a more selective and deliberate process: one integrates the perceived persona of the other without fully adopting their identity. The goal is not to become the other person, but to interact with an idealized, though partial, form of consciousness, a glorified embodiment of the other's being.

The Role of the Social Buffer

Central to this moderated integration is the concept of the social buffer. The social buffer is a psychological criterion that acknowledges, first and foremost, that the person with whom one is interacting is never the full extent of their consciousness. In other words, every interaction is not truly by way of a person's entire consciousness, but rather an embodied fragment of it, a particular possibility of consciousness, but never its full scope.

Secondly, one must recognize that, despite the consciousness the other individual may embody, it is intricately rooted in their unique fabric of existence; a complex dynamic shaped by their experiences, relationships, and countless other factors. Adapting that consciousness would be impossible because one would need access to the entire history of their development, including their lineage, experiences, relationships, and more, an impossibility.

Thirdly, the individual possesses a different set of dynamic experiences from our own. To truly understand them, one would need to deconstruct and challenge their own patterns of thought and development, reinterpreting those elements through this new perspective of consciousness. This requires a degree of self-denial and a willingness to step outside of one's own developmental process in order to grasp the other's perspective.

This recognition leads to three critical roles for the social buffer:

1. Recognizing the Partiality of Other's Consciousness

The buffer ensures that individuals understand anyone they encounter as a limited expression of consciousness. No one person can encapsulate the entirety of another's being. Their interactions are always with a fragment, a possibility of consciousness, rather than its totality. This understanding allows them to value the other person without risking complete absorption.

2. Regarding the Unique Developmental Fabric

Every individual's existence results from a complex interplay of dynamics: their experiences, relationships, and personal history create an inimitable model of development. The social buffer acknowledges that adopting another's consciousness entirely is impossible without erasing the very elements that define their individuality. It thus maintains a deference for the unique developmental history inherent in each person.

3. Preserving One's Own Dynamical Flow

Finally, the social buffer protects the integrity of one's advance. Fully integrating another's persona without reservation would require disrupting the natural developmental process; forcing a reinterpretation of one's experiences and denying established subjective flow. The buffer prevents such disfigurement, allowing for selective incorporation without self-denial.

There exists a dynamic interplay between admiration and self-preservation. While the domestication of consciousness involves adopting elements of another's identity, this process is tempered by an acute awareness of its limitations. Such selective integration is only possible through the mediation provided by the social buffer, a safeguard that distinguishes thriving interpersonal integration from pathological codependency.

The first insight, which each individual represents only a partial embodiment of consciousness, underscores the impossibility of ever fully adopting another's essence. Doing so would require a complete replication of their developmental history and intrinsic complexities. This recognition forms the bedrock of a balanced approach, ensuring that while one can draw inspiration from or even incorporate elements of another's persona, the sanctity of one's individuality remains intact.

II.3 Consciousness, Memory, and Interaction

Interactiveness and Domestication

Interactiveness and domestication are distinct processes. While they share some elements, they serve different functions. Domestication is the validation of parts for their own sake, whereas interactiveness involves the differentiation of consciousness. In simpler terms, domestication represents a separation from animated consciousness; while interactiveness refers to the elements of what was once a unified and wholesome nature of consciousness.

Both processes involve memory, but interactiveness memory serves as a bridge, helping to complete the integrity of consciousness. Conversely, domestication involves communication with a memory of consciousness that is received in its particles, allowing for personal interaction independent of the emanation of consciousness.

Memory afforded to domestication may not be immediately obvious. At first, it may seem that there is no memory involved, but rather the validation of the parts as they are. These parts, though rooted in consciousness, are detached from the whole. What remains, are the subdivisions most closely associated with the individual or group, recognized for their own sake. Memory can be traced if we carefully analyze and extract the data.

Child's Bag Example

For example, consider a child's bag. It is based on the child's memory of seeing an adult with their own bag, though this may not be apparent at first. Instead, it may seem like a softened version of a "bag" presently made suitable for the child.

The child interacts with the bag, or rather, actualizes it, as though they were an adult. The reason the child cannot fully accept this memory is due to a false premise; that they are not the adult. Thus, the bag becomes a hybrid of both adult and child elements. This bag has been domesticated, but it is not yet an interactive element.

In this example, the bag, within the broader system of representation in a civilized context, will be understood through its parts once the connection is severed. For instance, the handle of the bag represents the function of carrying things between two locations, or the traveling aspect; what we might call the "house between houses." These elements are only seen as interactive when isolated from the whole representation. Of course, these elements are embedded within the whole representation, but they are only truly noticed when differentiated and embodied. The bag itself was not created by a "need for a house between houses," but rather by the bag as a representation. After interactive dissection, we can understand how these elements contribute to the overall consciousness.

To illustrate this point, let's imagine removing the concept of "houses" entirely, leaving no representation of "house between houses." In this scenario, the bag as a representation is lost from our perspective. Picture a post-apocalyptic world, where the bag no longer stands out because there is no house on either side of it. Without the representation, the interactive elements that serve the partial duties of the structure also fade.

In the interactive view, the bag represents the memory of consciousness. In contrast, in the example with the child's bag, it represents the memory of leadership within domestication. The child's bag could also become a conscious element, but in this case, we are observing it from outside the system of consciousness.

Every interactive system requires a preloaded memory of consciousness to function and interact with its elements. In contrast, every domestication has a form that is more general and wholesome but remains connected to something separate from consciousness. The adult bag, in this case, is still disconnected from consciousness because it holds no representation other than its utility. However, the adult engages with the bag in response to an external system of consciousness. When consciousness no longer perceives bags as representations, such as in a post-apocalyptic world; adults will not use the bag in a way that lacks complete utility, and as a result, there would be no need for that domestication.

For instance, adults may wash clothes, but we do not see a domesticated version where children perform a simulated version of washing. Washing clothes is utilitarian, and there is no continued consciousness sentiment tied to it, so no domestication is required. However, clothes do undergo domestication because adults follow fashion trends, which creates the need for a domesticated version.

As a general rule, functions rooted in complete utility are not based on consciousness sentiment, while functions not tied to utility will be performed because of a consciousness sentiment, one which requires domestication. In line with our definition, domestication validates simpler versions of elements they can synchronize. The child's mind already contains an internal formulation of the sentiment attached to the adult's bag, derived from the external world. Without imposition, the child enters into communion with the elements tied to that sentiment. In this way, the child grasps the consciousness experience of the bag without external interference. This is a validation of an already existing conscious sentiment, now manifesting to complete the evidence chain.

Wholesome Domestication

A wholesome domestication does lack the pronounced individuality, even pertaining to the individual force of domestication. The wholesomeness follows the individual and their prior habitat of domestication according to all its differentiations. This allows for the full expression of individual domestication through the channels of one's vulnerabilities. By default, wholesome domestication not only accommodates individuality but also the vulnerabilities of that individuality across a certain spectrum and according to certain parameters. This leads to the demise of individual pronouncement. One cannot express their profound individuality when their vulnerabilities are exposed. Thus, during wholesome domestication, one loses wholesome individuality, and by having wholesome individuality, one loses wholesome domestication.

Genuine vitality is only possible when one does not seek to validate their existing components but rather leads from those existing components toward a new realm. When one validates their existing components, they must differentiate them to partake in a particular sense. Because of that, one cannot be wholesome; rather, differentiating into systematic parts allows for interactivity and thus domestication. Wholesome investigation occurs when the partialities of one system undergo a validating process that is wholesome, to include many of those particular aspects.

II.4 Social Constructs and Domesticated Structures

Consciousness in Social Constructs

Domestication is a powerful construct that, while often resembling the corporeal structure, is in fact part of the consciousness continuum. It does not isolate itself to fulfill a conscious function. Within a domesticated structure, there is a direct permeation of consciousness, all without reverting to its basic elements. This is its vulnerability: it must engage with direct consciousness while remaining secluded from proper formalization; an outcome of the broadness of consciousness, which is not directly accessible to the social individual.

Domestication sets the parameters for diluting consciousness into specific individuation, according to the rules of embodied experience; relatability. The familial body is the quintessential domesticated structure, given the familiarity of biological attachments and its semblance to a once-developing human form. Even an adopted family forms a potent domesticated structure due to this resemblance, which supports the perception of biological intimacy. This resemblance constitutes a perceptual individuation of self, supported by a strong relatability system; allowing one to experience those elements as nearly internal, without violating their external form.

The objective of domestication is precisely this: to create a potent capacity for individuation by accessing the sociality of the human being through their biological experience of selfhood. In doing so, it facilitates a diminutive version of consciousness that remains relatable to the human interface.

If we follow the specific details of the domesticated construct; for example, the childhood toy that resembles its correlation and infrastructure; we see that the child engages with the toy through an experience of infrastructure, without incorporating the wholeness of that infrastructure. Instead, the child gains the possibility of experiencing what it would be like to be part of the toy, without the complex, broader function of consciousness. When they play with the toy, they are not outside of consciousness; rather, they become part of the conscious sequence. There is nothing separate between the toy and its parallel in infrastructure; only that it is diluted and consequently relatable. It is not diminutive in the sense of losing the materiality of direct access to consciousness.

Even for the adult, the toy presents itself as part of the infrastructure. In fact, we find an adult infatuation with toys or childhood paraphernalia that goes beyond the child's initial interest. These toys are not merely tools for a process separate from consciousness; rather, they serve a diminutive function within consciousness itself. Their fault lies in forfeiting the all-encompassing nature of consciousness in favor of relatability.

Thus, this is the general role of all domesticated properties: they forfeit the broad, all-encompassing connections that make up the full spectrum of consciousness in order to access an individuated aspect. At the far end of the spectrum lies a forfeiture of far-reaching connections, resulting in a highly individualized, and therefore highly relatable; experience, but with limited participation in the broader field of consciousness.

This very process causes the domesticated structure to retain its systematic overlay within the psyche, despite one's continuing progression. A domesticated form will reassert itself at any stage of life. It resides, as it were, in the place where it first developed its structure, and it remains there, unchanged, throughout the psyche's lifetime.

For example, if one discovers they have a child they did not know about, they immediately enter into a domesticated structure, not according to any formalization of memory (because there was no memory beforehand), but because of attributes that were afforded a domesticated entity based on the idealization of having a child throughout the psyche. There is already a domesticated structure of a hypothetical child, which has now been filled by the news. Much like how young girls will play with dolls and role-play motherhood, they are already building the domesticated structure of motherhood; so, in some essence, or at least psychologically, they have already built a construct for motherhood and therefore are, in some sense, mothers.

Domesticated Corporeal Construct

When they reach the stage of genuine motherhood, they will, in fact, reach out to that developed domesticated structure within their psyche and utilize that framework within the realistic context of their life. That formalization of a domesticated structure lays dormant without change unless a very specific set of practices disrupts the construct.

This contrasts with the corporeal structure, which, in a competent setting, will not have any direct formalization in one's psyche as a memory construct, but rather as an objective process of activity. Once the motivation for that activity is set aside, the corporeal construct dissipates. Although there is a general structure by which one will approach all corporeal constructs based on how they understand such an approach, this is rooted in their understanding, and any further development in that understanding will change the structure.

This is in contrast to the domesticated construct, which simply remains as it is despite understanding, so that one who has reached intellectual strides will still, in fact, retain the domesticated structures that have lain dormant within their psyche as if they were in their most perennial state. All of a sudden, they could act out the full formalization of what it would be like to be a child, because it retains its viability without change.

The practices that do enable a structural change to a domesticated construct are, in fact, only two: one is exhaustive domestication, and the other is existential detachment from the domesticated construct. Exhaustive domestication is the more readily known and utilized, and when enacted, it enables the conversations and sociality that have been retained in the construct of that domesticated content. In its further stage of constant interaction, it eventually confines itself and loses its variability.

Much like how a family body that separates from the outside world will, in its primary stage, do well. But over time, because of its lack of connection to the consciousness spectrum, will start to exhaust itself to the point where the emotional contents mute themselves. Until, in some sense, there is nothing left other than the possibility of it becoming a corporeal construct, with its members now merely part of that construct and not domesticated in any context.

The moment a domesticated construct exhausts itself and retains its structure, it transitions into a corporeal construct; which, by and large, is not necessarily a problem but simply the recognition of that transition. We do find a certain distaste for the experience of a family body revolving into a corporeal construct because it loses its semblance of direct relatability and its homage to the aspects that domestication exemplifies. But, in fact, a corporeal construct is a significant process in the general experience of consciousness for what it serves and a family body requires a divergence to a corporeal construct to contribute an outline and semblance to perceive, despite its domesticated prowess.

When a domesticated construct transitions into a corporeal construct, it no longer serves as a helm for conscious reception but rather as a formalization of contextual interactions, based on the ability to perform as a corporeal construct. In the case of a family body, when it transitions into a corporeal construct, it could be that the entire corporeal construction is to ensure a domesticated quality; even though that quality is no longer accessible by virtue of corporeal separation from consciousness, at least from direct consciousness.

The exhaustion process is based on the sociality of the reception of direct consciousness. If there is a reception of more direct consciousness, or if the sociality develops in a deeper sequence to vitalize that sociality, then it would not be exhaustible. Direct consciousness is its remedy; the process by which any domestication can be revitalized. Therefore, memory-based or indirect consciousness alone will not suffice; without direct consciousness, exhaustion is inevitable. Even if there were a memory-based finalization of consciousness, and the domesticated construct followed that memory, it would still lack the vitality that only direct consciousness provides.

Almost the opposite of a corporeal construct, in which; without the indirect connection of consciousness that remains adrift and does not actualize into the direct connection; the entire corporeal construct degenerates. This is the case with the domesticated construct, where, without direct interactions with consciousness, it will not be vitalized enough to enable the sociality of memory-based or indirect consciousness and will ultimately be exhausted.

Unlike a corporeal construct, which degenerates and loses its viability as a formal setting, the domesticated construct simply exhausts itself. Any further attempts will restructure into a corporeal construct or, if further pursued as a domesticated property, become a problematic construct akin to a cult-like system.

To illustrate these ideas, let's consider a standard couple. In their early stages, their relationship is fully embedded in a domesticated process; being that it assumes direct interactions with consciousness, as the entire romantic endeavor is based on attachment to consciousness systems. This is embodied in the developing couple. In this case, they are a formalization of a domesticated construct, to which it has a sociability that embodies the individuation of consciousness, and we will not consider the circumstance to be a corporeal construct in any manner.

For the couple to become exhaustible, they would need to lose attachment to direct consciousness. For if they continuously engender their coupling in association with direct consciousness, so long as it remains direct consciousness, it will be in-exhaustible; although other problems can arise that are beyond this present conversation. Now, in order to make them exhaustible, we need to sever the direct attachment to consciousness. This can happen through distance from interaction with consciousness, or it can occur when the relatability within that social system deepens to the point where it begins to perceive itself as beyond consciousness, essentially treating itself as a self-contained conscious system.

It is a domesticated construct that now assumes a proprietary role instead of merely a receptive one; in other words, it takes on an ego of its own, causing them to become detached from the direct connection to consciousness. If the initial stages of that romance continued unabated, without the individuation or assertion of their domesticated quality, they would remain connected to direct consciousness as long as they remain in proximity to it.

Moreover, there is the general accession to any domesticated system for exhausting itself by virtue of basing its sociality upon its internal construct without separation or deviation. The couple that begins its later stages of romance may begin to become unavailable to the detachment of that domesticated system, so that in their attempt to access direct interaction, they will be riddled with the domesticated quality that they have not fully disentangled. This occurs by virtue of the very fact that they are constantly enabling the domesticated construct, to then lose that ability to detach from its existential parameters.

In this way, they begin to lose direct attachment to consciousness because of the existential attachment of the domesticated construct, so that we are beginning to see the defeat can either be of the quality and external access, or from the internality and its existential attachment, to which then access to consciousness begins to become limited.

At the eventual climax, this domesticated construct begins to exhaust itself; the sociality does not partake in any formalization or individuation of consciousness. It either becomes, much like the general process experienced by mature couples; a condition for which the corporeal construct serves as a remedy, as seen in institutions such as marriage or childbearing, or other such formalizations that engage the corporeal system and thereby avoid the usual rules of exhaustion.

There is another element at play, which; besides the direct interaction of consciousness as the parameter of exhaustion; is the level of sociality based on that experience. In the case of complex devotion to sociality, it extends the permeability of that consciousness interaction so that the individuation becomes enlarged.

In the case of diluted direct access to consciousness; and we could say that in any construct there would be some access; the final product is only based on what level of sociality it has developed. If the domesticated construct is simply the most viable details of consciousness embodiment, exhaustion is much closer. But if it were in the case of expansive qualities of such individuation, so that the sociality embodies a complex arena of details to the individuation of that consciousness, it could be the case that despite the diminutive access to consciousness, it can still construct itself as a domesticated element because the details have been extracted at that level of organization.

In our case, it is the revelation of whatever access is contingent upon the organization, which then follows a credence that leads to an experience of individuation, allowing for a wholesome experience of consciousness.

We could take, for example, a prison; to which all would agree has lost a very strong degree of direct access to consciousness; but still can be a successful endeavor if the sociality develops in proportion to its loss of direct access to consciousness. For even in a prison cell, one can access a relatability construct that retains a very potent degree of whatever consciousness remains accessible.

This is a general rule in all of consciousness: a larger scale can always be diluted if only the expanded parts in proportion give credence to its weaker construct. In the case of the prison, one can view the walls in precise relatability, so that they re-access the losses of that direct consciousness; much like how a highway would serve the general public, this wall serves the incarcerated individual in achieving a domesticated quality.

Sociality's Buffer Role in Conscious Decline

Sociality plays a critical role in this dynamic. Attachment to sociality carries expectations, demands that facilitate interaction between these domains. When one detaches from sociality, the agent of encapsulation and the link to domestication; this buffer disappears, and the individual is forced to choose between two extremes: total domestication or complete de-domestication. Institutions such as marriage, along with broader societal expectations surrounding domestication, mediate this interaction between the psyche's domains.

In a domesticated context, when the sociality which supports domestication is removed; as in the case of a family unit isolated from broader social structures; this mediation disappears. The family must then return to exposure to revitalize the space. Rather than deepening domestication, encapsulation becomes a mechanism to fill the void left by the absence of external mediation.

The extraterrestrial endeavor does not originate from a domesticated region of the psyche reaching into its external counterpart. Instead, it results from an incomplete domestication process. The external domain becomes the sole source of vitality. This explains why a family unit may fail to domesticate surrounded by a sociality lacking the necessary nuance: without a social buffer to mediate, any domain they inhabit lacks vitality, as though the shadow of their surroundings suffocates them.

Sociality provides simultaneous stimulation, acting as an external mediator for interactions without necessarily producing genuine consciousness. It offers just enough simulation to allow domestication to persist. However, when sociality weakens or shifts, this stimulation fades, and the transfer of vitality from a domain no longer aligned with the external world begins to dissipate.

Another critical role of sociality is the mediation of psychological material between domains. Social frameworks enable the interaction of the psyche's components through the process of domestication, which, in turn, becomes a ruminative sentiment. The danger of domestication lies in its failure to fulfill this mediating role. Without it, the environment devolves into a non-domesticated space, or into one where domestication becomes disconnected from rumination.

Roles fulfill expectations, and when either the expectations themselves (their specific parameters) or the sociality that upholds them is lost, the framework necessary for internal psychic interaction collapses. The second clause, sociality conveying the expectation; depends on recognition and attachment to a sociality that delivers those experiences. If sociality begins to dismiss certain tenets, domestication erodes. If it adopts additional parameters, the individual becomes further entrenched in domestication.

Finally, sociality is not bound to a linear progression emerging from encapsulation, but rather depends on it. In cases of extreme aversion to exposure, sociality may offer contradictory parameters, further entrenching domestication and obstructing interaction among the psyche's various parts, as one part may come to be seen as hostile.

II.5 THE COMPLEXITY OF DOMESTICATION: SOCIAL AND PSYCHOLOGICAL REFLECTIONS

A domesticated setting mirrors one's internal state across the social spectrum. It becomes more sophisticated when there is a higher degree of diversity in that sociality, making simple validation of accepted norms and logical inferences insufficient for engineering such a system. We might even encounter an extreme case where an accepted domestication, defined as the gathering for amelioration; would not be allowed, either for fear of a final outcome of further differentiation, or because the agreement does not include all aspects of participation. One would not sit in a domesticated setting alongside an enemy, for then the roles of friend and foe become convoluted. In other terms, the adherence to what makes them an enemy becomes more important than what makes them similar. For example, a group that thinks alike, despite its numbers contributing to the perspective in that particular domicile, would transform to a simpler form of domestication, like that of a singular couple, or even less.

We can mirror this with personal or psyche domestication, where one's internal thoughts, which naturally manifest, can be the cause of either simple matters (like the validation of thoughts that are rummaging the brain in response to current events), or more complex matters, where there is a manifestation from past experiences combined with current developments. In this case, a diverse range of states from one's life are embedded together in a natural conversation, without active participation. The domesticated content is not validating itself, but rather providing a format to integrate these diverse aspects, ultimately leading to amelioration.

We find the same format when we have a complex and diverse group participating in domestication. Despite the aspects that separate them, they are brought together to consolidate across that spectrum. We can define these terms as follows: validation refers to the mirroring of thoughts according to a greater sociality, and consolidation is a complex form of validation where opposition exists at every interval until amelioration takes place.

II.6 SHIFTS IN CONSCIOUSNESS AND DOMESTICATION

The Process of Domestication in Consciousness Changes

When there is a major change in consciousness, whether through a change of location or life events; before any therapeutic mending can be attempted, there needs to be a domestication of affairs. A change in consciousness is also considered a revamp of the entire system, so that any previously recorded consciousness is laid dormant, allowing the new consciousness to take effect. This domestication allows for the interactivity of prior states of consciousness to mediate and permeate throughout the new state of consciousness. Domestication does not occur immediately after the conscious shift, but only through an attempt to approach the new consciousness and recognize the need for domestication.

This need for domestication is based on the degree of exposure and does not follow the normal circumstance of domestication; instead, it slowly disseminates its information throughout the psyche. The purpose of domestication is not to retain information merely for the sake of it, but rather, it is the initial exposure that allows for interactivity between the self and prior consciousness states.

For instance, travel is a change in consciousness because the locales influence the consciousness system, especially through personal associations. The destination will be a consciousness exposure that cannot be mended because interactivity has yet to be located. First, one must undergo a domestication of that perceptual sentiment so that the consciousness material permeates the psyche at a personal level, making it available to be mended.

Embodied vs. Private Domestication

This is not embodied domestication, which can only occur once there has been private domestication.

One can theoretically embody domestication through the mechanisms of a social organization, much like the *embodied interactive locale*. However, this fails to engage at the individual level if the material has not yet reached sufficient depth; there is, therefore, no relatability. There is a common temptation to pursue embodied interactivity in place of private interactivity. Embodied interactivity appears in many forms; such as the family body, religious practice, and other collective models that offer approximations of what it might feel like to experience domestication.

The family body, being the primary site of domestication; only functions evocatively when there has already been a domestication of one's individual and private affairs. At that point, a certain level of embodiment becomes necessary to ascend the hierarchy of interactivity. At its base lies private interactivity. If this foundational level is not cultivated, the higher layers and echelons of interactivity cannot be sustained. The lowest level must be prioritized first and most, with each subsequent layer of embodiment building upon it.

If one comes into the family body as a kind of therapeutic or compensatory experience, without prior individuation and private investigation; then the attention required for genuine domestication is lost. Instead of being domesticated, the experience becomes merely a conscious event. This is the common misstep: actualizing the family body as an encapsulation of consciousness rather than allowing it to become a receptacle of invited domestication. Without a proper foundation, the family body loses its function as an embodied medium and becomes only a conscious encapsulation, one devoid of prior domestication.

II.7 Breakdown and Recovery of Consciousness

Breakdown via Fixation and Oppression

There are two perspectives on the active use of domestication, each concerning what lies beyond it. The first is cultic dedication, where the premise of domestication serves its own purpose, with the stipulation that the dedication is directed toward a specific, unnamed context. For example, the dedication of a home serves the personal, private aspect of an individual's life, one that does not need to intersect with public experience, such as defecation, hygiene, sleep, or basic nourishment.

However, the dedication itself does not inherently carry this meaning. It merely refers to the container for a specific objective, which could, in theory, have near-infinite applications. Yet, these possibilities are largely theoretical, as the individual psyche tends to narrow its focus on what constitutes the connotation of dedication. The dedication, regardless of introspection, will define itself as the habitat for whatever the psyche deems most pressing; an issue requiring stabilization and integration. For instance, if one's unmediated consciousness is primarily concerned with a specific learning development (e.g., learning to read or understand the alphabet), they will naturally orient itself in that direction to facilitate the necessary mediation.

In the case of cultic dedication, assuming the majority of unintegrated consciousness dominates the localized integration, the individual does not regulate or oversee the process. They merely provide the measure of dedication and await the psyche to proceed accordingly with a contextual performance. However, this approach allows for the potential of mislaid procedure, as one consents to the disillusionment of the inner process. After the dedication occurs, any consequential event, whether mental or environmental, will trigger a specific aspect of consciousness to be mediated.

This route might seem extended, as instead of directly addressing the primary concern, one passes through subsequent layers. Eventually, the most pressing mediation will reveal itself. However, this approach is not foolproof. For instance, there is the issue of over-dedication. After fulfilling the necessary dedication, a continuation of dedication can reintroduce the objective's premise, preventing true domestication. Rather than allowing the domestication process to unfold naturally, one remains in motion toward regenerating the system, rather than simply allowing it to function.

Degeneration and Identity Collapse

If dedication reaches its culmination, and the objective of domestication finally takes effect, the psyche, whether individually or socially; may take the path of least resistance, leading to the most pressing mediations that require the most effort. The very reason these issues remain unmediated (such as trauma) is precisely due to their intensity. These issues will remain unresolved unless actively processed. In their natural state, under the influence of dedication, individuals may instead focus on inconsequential but stimulating aspects, which provide the necessary stimulation for the domestication process.

Thus, one may find themselves repeatedly mediating specific aspects of consciousness that seem extraneous to the psyche's process but are enough to maintain the sentiment of that domicile. If this continues in a long-lasting state, the entire premise of the domestication process becomes destabilized, seeking out niche aspects of consciousness that reflect upon themselves, rather than focusing on the majority aspect of the psyche. By insisting on following the niche; whether by deliberate choice or due to the path of least resistance, the psyche begins to reflect upon itself.

In any case of fixation, whether psychological, social, or constructive; when there is little stimulatory response from continued association, one will begin to perceive the object of interest not for itself, but as a mirror of the psyche. Take, for example, oral fixation. The vantage point will not view the oral aspect for itself, but through a worldview in which the oral realm is dominant. Within this system, muted avatars receive the experience of oral interactions, all contained within that specific realm. In this instance, instead of considering the oral fixation as a standalone feature, one treats it as the center of a larger, self-contained universe. Over time, this sociality becomes more complex, as it reflects other socialities, creating a feedback loop where the system's complexity grows.

To facilitate this process, lower-level avatars emerge to reflect upon the aspect of fixation. These avatars, however, will remain in negative contrast to the system. There is no inclination to reflect positively upon the system itself, as the realm is self-contained. As a result, all reflections of this system will be coerced into action, reflecting only the shadow of the fixation.

This overextension toward stimulating aspects results in the psyche receiving the experience of its negative attributes. The entire endurance depends on reflecting upon the system's failure, which generates symptoms of fixation. In this process, the fixated realm draws one into its interactive material, exploring how it retains its vulnerability. Thus, a psyche becomes permeated with negative connotations toward the fixation, while continuing to adhere to it.

Under such dominion, where one is subservient to the system, the receptacles contrast themselves in a negative connotation. The consciousness that allowed the fixation to begin may relate back to the entire fixation process as a shadow in itself, with no understanding of how it should be stimulated for the process. Now, this may seem like the perfect end to a psychological malady, but in fact, it is the furthest degeneration. Not only is there a system of affairs filled with the contrast of itself, without recognition of how it proceeds as a purposeful agenda, but the entire consciousness system beyond the fixation, through which it allowed the fixation to start; begins to lose its grounding as part of the psyche. In the end, both the initiation of the fixation and the fixation itself lose their authority.

We can observe this in regular social circumstances, where an oppressor continuously oppresses until the subservient sociality contrasts to such a level of negativity that the oppressor themselves begins to view their enterprise through the lens of how they are perceived. Eventually, they lose any stimulation to continue that process but, in their full degeneration, although broken from the possibility of continuing oppression; lose their anchor to the way they were before the oppression took place.

Consequently, the subservient avatars or social aspects will have no ground to stand on, as their entire enterprise was in contrast to the oppressor, who is now unavailable. The oppressor cannot return to its higher system because it has lost its footing as an enterprise by losing its identification. Thus, the entire system shatters; not only the oppressive role but the entire realm that allowed for the oppression to take place. Extreme oppression at a state level can lead to the degeneration of the entire state.

In the psychological context, fixation can cause an individual to lose their connection to the rest of the psyche's experience, leading to a loss of consciousness regarding the identification of the superego that governs the fixation. Coupled with a loss of that identification, this leads to existential pandemonium; not the consciousness preceding the fixation, but a disparity of loss and indifference.

The only remedy for this breakdown is the recollection of the final moment when the fixation receded as a superego dominion. When the oppressor finally falls, the holder of this memory is neither the oppressor nor the subservient force, but the all-encompassing consciousness that preceded the fixation. This memory serves as the gateway back to conscious sentiment, as it is not obliterated but lacks a defined identity. In the case of a societal oppressor, this memory serves as a foundation for reclaiming agency and stability.

The ending of one process can only serve as the beginning of another in the case where there is adherence to that gateway. Any attempt to access consciousness through another route will lack the necessary infrastructure to support it. After an oppressor's decline, there is no reassertion of that exact role. Instead, sub-modalities of the oppressor's influence take their place, those who were once subservient; embodying a reclusive consciousness. However, the system that once existed is no longer the same, as the identities that follow are inherently less potent.

In the psychological context, the decline of a fixation will not be followed by its reassertion but rather by the emergence of a new fixation. This arises not from the object of fixation itself, but from the reclusive consciousness seeking an identity holder. The only way to prevent this cycle is access to the moment when the fixation receded, allowing the psyche to disengage from its hold.

The Greeks conquered the Romans not by force, but through existential dominance. Over time, the Romans were transformed into Greeks, and the Greco-Roman influence became inseparable in historical discourse. Similarly, once an oppressor is understood and their underlying motivations recognized, they lose their existential status. This understanding breaks the cycle of oppression, rendering the oppressor's physical domination inconsequential. In this way, they maintain that access and are not considered subservient in their existential state, because they remain in the modality of subservience; even while they acknowledge the expansive consciousness behind the identity held by the oppressor.

In some ways, an oppressor is dissolved simply by understanding them and what lies behind their actions. This understanding creates a sense of possibility that prevents the oppressor from continuing to exert control, as one no longer sees them in the same way. Consequently, the oppressor loses their existential status as an authority and becomes merely a physical force of inconsequential nature.

This brings us back to domestication; not in its dedication, but in the way that dedication allows for a specific objective. Through dedication, one becomes available to what lies beyond domestication, but only through the domesticated realm itself. Rather than relying on the existential causation of domestication via cultic dedication, one can regulate the process through psychic choice; directing the focus to objectives that lie beyond the realm of domestication. Although still guided by the path of least resistance, this process is controlled through directed disjunction. Moreover, in all the possibilities of being under the dominion of that dedication, relying on the ensuing existential reality; one controls the process, at least in the existential realm. Eventually, the physical realm will reflect itself, and the oppressor will recede in being existentially inconsequential.

II.8 PERSISTENT DOMESTICATED COMPLEXES

Oedipus Complex and Lifelong Impact

The Oedipus complex is but one of multitudes of domesticated systems within the developing psyche. Because it constitutes a preliminary domestication, in the case where a psyche processes later developments as participants of conscious experience or contextual regard, the prior domesticated entities remain dormant as they were; without negotiation or development. They simply sit as they are, so that in the case of regulating current individuation toward stepwise satiation of regular consciousness, these domesticated systems will begin to set the criteria of direction.

Not always does a domesticated system take part in one's experience with regular consciousness, but it does so if unattended; attempting to triangulate the domesticated property in command for public exposure, to assist its development. This is akin to having a genuine home, or being a homebody; where, although one moves toward communion with public rumination, it is not necessarily the case that such domestication will be the influential factor. Still, we cannot be sure that at some point it would not begin to shape the course of one's systemic development, simply because it seeks either to disintegrate or integrate, or to evolve its aspects alongside regular consciousness.

There is always an aspect of individuation that contrasts with consciousness. That dynamic will be fashioned by the prior domesticated elements of one's development, and the Oedipus complex will take charge if it remains underdeveloped or not properly established.

In the other scenario, the Oedipus complex is a domesticated construct under which all processes of the psyche continue; within its domain. While adulthood may be viewed as an experience of development, with the Oedipus complex defining its nuances and details, it lacks a superior pronouncement of itself, because one has not fully departed from that complex. Thus, in all their informational relay, the system seeks public exposure from within its internal base; though, most of the time, its internal domain will negate any incoming data that might seek to reflect it.

In this case as well, there is only a minimal experience of public exposure outside the domesticated realm, since the system has been partialized to maintain adherence to that complex.

Even if one were to elaborate the domesticated complex to its near-infinite degree, approaching all its nuances with academic sophistication; or exploring the bitter ends of the Oedipus complex and its ramifications; it still would not supersede the entity or exhaust its favors, simply because it is such a preliminary complex that the psyche cannot fully exhaust it.

We might think that if such were possible, one would reach a stage of development where the ramifications of the Oedipus complex would no longer be detailed in their evolution, but we fail to see that play out. All the metaphors noted by Freud and his contemporaries, such as Melanie Klein, in which the Oedipus complex unfolds during adolescence, continue unabated throughout lifetimes, serving the ongoing conversation of the Oedipus complex without deviation.

Thus, we have before us two equations: One is the expansion of a domesticated complex without deviation into public exposure, but at the cost of nuance and experience beyond it. This could be seen as the somewhat sufficient development of a domesticated complex, all without engaging other systems.

On the other hand, we have the option for neglecting attention toward domesticated complexes, focused solely on the public experience of consciousness. In this scenario, these domesticated complexes begin to participate in the individuation of that interaction, such that consciousness itself becomes detailed by these domesticated complexes.

This, in itself, may not be a problem; if we understand that a certain domesticated complex is not necessarily the requisite form of interaction for all of consciousness, but only as much as it serves a contextual mainframe.

The solution to the domesticated complex is internal development, existential separation, and experience with consciousness separate from that complex; so that all will serve each other in their proper time.

In the example mentioned, the Oedipus complex is only perfected when it is first allowed internal development in accordance with later public exposure and experience. This allows it to gain nuance from within its own affection; most reflecting the intimate nature of the domesticated complex itself. Then comes existential separation, allowing one to engage with consciousness without the burden of complexity. Finally, there is the return to the domesticated complex; so it can be utilized as a tool in the ongoing development of consciousness, serving as an archival system for extraction.

At no point does the Oedipus complex fall away from personhood; which cannot be said for all other domesticated complexes, as it depends on their level of existential participation in addition to the delicate development of the psyche.

For instance, in the experience of catastrophic events of global proportion, one might generate a domesticated complex which, despite everything said above, despite affirmation; still would not be exhausted for its extensional ramifications. It would be impossible for one to exhaust the domesticated complex of World War II, for example, for at least 50 years beyond the event, regardless of how they approach it.

Whether they approach it through internal development; remaining sedentary and empathetically engaging with the experience to gain nuanced growth; or whether they existentially separate to participate in consciousness and later return to adhere to that domesticated complex, even in perpetual cycles, it would not exhaust the complex and they would still reattribute themselves along the continuum of that element.

Consciousness itself, bearing the existential demarcation of the world war (or whatever locale one chooses to engage), has not developed beyond it; despite personal existential separation. Now, we can approach this from the angle of personal development, or personal existential imputation; which, despite one's existential separation, will maintain coherence in accordance with whichever manner one enters the consciousness continuum.

This usually happens during the initial years of life, as it is at this stage that all other development relies on and from which one can never fully depart. Even if one experiences that existential aspect later in life, the psyche retains such an imprint that any form of existential separation will only momentarily keep it at bay but will eventually resurface due to that foundational setting.

In the public realm, the reason World War II became imprinted as a domesticated complex in the years that followed is because, on an individual level, this was the case, and individuals, at a fundamental level, shape consciousness.

There are other catastrophic events that did not carry the same level of existential demarcation as World War II. For instance, World

War I did not form that same domesticated union for its generation. Whatever complex it did create was less defining, less concrete, as such, it is harder to define as an event

II.9 Symbolic and Material Expressions

Symbolism of Clothing in Domesticity and Publicness

There is a symbolic, and perhaps more direct relationship between the way we link clothing and the facilitation of movement between doorways or localities; whether physical or conceptual. This association arises in the communication between the internal settlement (the safety of home) and external movement, and it is represented through fashion. For instance, bags, coats, and other items associated with mobility. The internal realm and its expenditure do not require such elements; mobility is unnecessary because there is no requirement to change physical locations. Similarly, bags to carry items from one place to another are not needed, and climate is organized within any physical structure, one way or another.

Fashion often exists in extremes; such as home ground, represented by certain sweaters, and the general outdoors, represented by boots; where each serves a distinct purpose. Boots, while indoors, for example, carry an outdoor connotation, while certain sweaters worn outside yield a domesticated sensibility. Between these extremes lies the full spectrum of fashion. This spectrum contributes to our perception of clothing, as it acts as a marker of the external environment. Every item of fashion can be placed somewhere on this spectrum; domesticated with a slight degree of mobility, or utility with a slight degree of domestication. This is why the man's suit has remained a staple. It fulfills a degree of domestication; specifically, the "dinner jacket," which provides warmth and embodies domesticity of a controlled climate.

As Roland Barthes states in The Fashion System:

"The ludic nature of these utterances becomes quite apparent when they take an extreme form, which through its excess indicates the very limits of the system, i.e., of signification; in the famous little suit that looks like a suit (or even a very 'suit' suit), signification achieves its own paradox, it becomes reflexive: the signifier signifies itself." (Barthes, The Fashion System, 263).[4]

The outdoors, on the other hand, is a non-controlled climate, where a jacket might not serve its intended purpose. If the environment is extreme, additional material is needed. In perfect weather, however, one can do without an extra article of clothing.

Domestication is often associated with a presumed climate. From the time of the dinosaurs in caves, there was a basic understanding of the elements; just enough to address a slight chill. For warmth, a jacket could be put on, but in a public setting, one could not remove it so freely. Conversely, for the cold, the climate will be controlled externally.

The use of a single, unmitigated fabric for both pants (which are entirely utilitarian) and jackets (which serve a more domesticated purpose) demonstrates the corporeal nature of fashion. This is public domestication; a fine way to describe an institution or corporation. When pushed further, domestication takes on a familial tone. When public utility is involved, as in the case of an overcoat or more durable pants, or even the separation of fabrics; it suggests a connection to the outdoors. This duality is one reason the little suit has endured despite

---

[4] Roland Barthes, The Fashion System, trans. Matthew Ward and Richard Howard (New York: Hill and Wang, 1983), 263.

dramatic shifts in the fashion industry. The intersection between these two realms is too significant for a keen observer to overlook.

The sentiment toward either of these two elements reveals the criteria by which an individual is defined. When there is hostility toward outdoor representations, such as the imperfections between a jacket and suit pants; it suggests a lack of agreement with the public framework that gives domestication its conscious purpose. On the other hand, when there is hostility toward the jacket, particularly in summer heat, domestication is perceived as a confinement from which one must break free.

SECTION III: DOMESTICATING CONSCIOUSNESS AND ITS PITFALLS

III.1 Introducing Domesticated Consciousness

AUTHOR'S NOTATION:

This section is not the groundwork of domestication in its psychological and philosophical course, but rather the introduction of a new concept: that of domesticating consciousness. Whenever we refer to the process of domestication alongside consciousness, we are referring to this novel concept. We are not exploring the domesticated process, nor are we introducing the philosophical format of consciousness, but only in how domestication and consciousness interact, especially in its degenerative state.

To understand the process of domesticated consciousness, we must first understand domestication in general. Domestication involves the capability to actualize at a lower scale, allowing domestic elements to be applied without the full scope of consciousness. When one becomes attached to consciousness, seeking to create a *home* within it, not as separate from the habitat, but as a way to make consciousness itself "a home", One is not merely deeply interacting with consciousness; one is also imagining oneself as an entity capable of containing the full scope of consciousness as an applicable layer within their domesticated system.

At this point, the psychological process itself remains theoretical. Typically, individuals interact with the consciousness as an interactive force, seeking to actualize within its realm. But when one applies domestication in the interior of animated consciousness, they essentially become consciousness itself, rather than presenting as a sublayer that exists on top of the individual.

Because of this, they embody consciousness and simultaneously extinguish it. They become codependent on the conscious element, utilizing such as an eminence of reality. For reality is one in the same as consciousness for such an individual, and they will posture the wholeness of reality as if they were its platform. Though this may seem conceited, it is not, for a prideful individual believes themselves to embody traits that are more deficient than they demonstrate. We are describing a domesticated version of consciousness; a constructed form in which consciousness is compressed into an anatomical layer of the individual, lacking the necessary separation from its source. The psyche envelops with that data stream, leaving no other reserve for the possibility of interaction, or any other utility of the psyche for that matter. This creates the illusion of full intellectual capacity, while in reality, remaining only a fabricated version that mimics consciousness by embedding it directly into a bodily form.

III.2 DIRECT INTERACTION WITH CONSCIOUSNESS AND THE PROCESS OF DOMESTICATION

The process of domesticating consciousness advances when one interacts directly with consciousness in a way that exerts a domesticating effect. This means that instead of approaching conscious substance through a context, one goes directly to the source of consciousness. Rather than allowing consciousness to permeate the psyche with a significant regulatory effect, one takes the mantle of going directly to the permeation and distributing its contents throughout the psyche. This agency of attenuating to consciousness without any change to the psyche's requirement of disruption is what differentiates that from regular forms of domestication; hence, we term it as 'domesticating consciousness'; the act of domesticating is the differing factor. Consciousness, although permeable and substantial, cannot be directly domesticated nor interacted without separation and mediation.

When one interacts directly with consciousness without any domestication process, they do so without assigning a domain to contain that substance This has the benefit of distancing from it in contrast of direct interaction. Even the terminology of domesticity has the connotation of distance and separation, yet, that very process can be used as an agency for proximity and exposure.

Typically, the level of interaction corresponds to a contextual layer. For example, if someone is sophisticated with their interaction, they possess a context that facilitates it. If less sophisticated, they rely on the structural domain to provide that context. This reflects the evolution of consciousness advance: initially, all contact was domain-centered; the concrete domain became the first offering for interaction with consciousness, though this interaction can also occur as an internal process of the psyche as a *contextual* domain. However, one can manipulate or rather subvert the process so that instead of interacting under the auspices of a specific domain or contextual layer, they interact directly with consciousness.

At present this may seem impossible: where is the basis for interaction without acknowledging the domain that houses that very sentiment? Yet, although structurally incongruent, it is technically possible for the psyche. One can persuade the psyche, first, that domain settings are neither restrictive nor arbitrary, and second, rather than relying on context, one moves toward direct domesticity.

Although consciousness lacks a clear material form, as long as there is some social infrastructure transmitting its emanation, direct interaction is possible; provided it occurs in real time through that infrastructure. We cannot pinpoint a precise element that encloses consciousness, as it is both permeable and intangible, yet focused attention enables interaction even in the absence of domain-specific or contextual grounding.

Consciousness typically manifests through infrastructure, domains, and conceptual elements. However, one need not engage with these directly to interact with consciousness itself. That is, while consciousness is secured to context, one may bypass that layer and engage the substance directly.

For example, political certainties such as roads and governmental infrastructure practices are tangible domains that offer a form to conscious substance. The relevance of a specific governmental element or transportation portal depends on its contextual place in a broader system; its proximity to other locations, its functional role, and so on. This context lends shape and legitimacy to the conscious substance, such that anyone interacting with it directly will also encounter its embedded context. This might include structural domains (e.g., asphalt on a road) or abstract relations (e.g., the road connecting two domains). Either way, context shapes consciousness. Thus, even when one bypasses context to interact directly with consciousness, the contextual imprint persists.

Nonetheless, it is possible to engage consciousness directly, entering into communion without contextual mediation, though context may be reintroduced afterward. For instance, one may interact with a road as a conscious substance, disregarding its institutional or ideological associations, and in doing so, come into direct communion. In this state, one approximates unity with that consciousness. From here, one can proceed with that embodiment without further contextual reference; until the time comes to implant the context that gave rise to the substance. In our example, the individual may later recognize the road's contextual meaning by retracing their psychic movement from unity (totality) to conceptual understanding (approximation).

Children experience this naturally. Lacking education or awareness of contextual overlays, they often interact directly with consciousness, without parental guidance or the influence of the superego, becoming bound to the conscious substance itself. Later in life, retracing is often required: to reinterpret premature conscious experiences through their proper context, seeing parents not as omnipotent beings, but as physical structures and social instruments of domestication. This disruption is not merely about changing interpretations of parental figures; it arises from premature interactions with their associated consciousness; interactions that subverted traditional contexts deeply enmeshed in the individual.

There are risks to becoming excessively approximate to consciousness. It can result in disassociation from its true nature, or a fractured psyche unable to maintain coherence. There is also the hazard of perceiving consciousness as a totality, without acknowledging its contextual origin. One cannot bargain with consciousness to determine its limits; instead, one often assumes such as its composite whole.

Having addressed the capacity to engage consciousness directly, we turn to domestication and distribution; how conscious substance becomes embedded and processed in the psyche. Typically, interaction with consciousness occurs through context. But on occasion, it happens directly. Regardless, this leads to an encapsulation; a form of conscious imprint layered onto the psyche. A necessary process follows, in which this encapsulation is distributed across differentiated parts of the psyche. This is domestication.

Domestication generally takes place in private, away from public expression. It dilutes and fragments conscious matter to make it manageable. Because the conscious substance is enlarged and indivisible, it cannot be distributed as-is; it must be processed in stages. Still, one may attempt to domesticate consciousness while in direct contact with it; encapsulating and distributing the experience prematurely. But this does not fundamentally work. A whole, undifferentiated consciousness cannot be mapped cleanly onto fragmented psychic parts.

Despite this, the effort persists. One takes general consciousness and reinterprets it to fit into domesticated forms. This reinterpretation is not the true nature of the experience, but a version of it that can be managed contained by the psyche. Since the *whole* cannot be layered as-is, some strive to preserve it by separating it from the domesticated layers altogether.

Faced with this dilemma, the psyche often replaces the wholesome experience at every level of the organization with a version that mimics its wholeness, stripped of original form, tailored to fit internal criteria. This is why those who regularly domesticate consciousness often gravitate toward political realities: they provide an accessible framework for reinterpreting consciousness at every level of psychic domestication.

Children, for instance, intuitively recognize political structures by perceiving infrastructure. It's as if one gains partial insight into every form of consciousness, but only at its political layer. If the consciousness is of literary form, the interaction is filtered through canonical texts; if scientific, it is mediated through institutional discourse. In all these cases, the interpreted elements function socially but lack independence, embedded as they are in broader systemic contexts. Thus, the conscious experience remains inauthentic, even at the political level.

III.3 THE REJECTION OF SELF AND SOCIETY

Domesticating consciousness will still be a domesticated process, albeit with a "consciousness overhead"; more so than regular domestication, which, in whatever degree of expansion, will not take over the portion of the psyche attributed to consciousness itself or, more specifically, to the external manifestation of consciousness. This, then, is the cause of d-consciousness (domesticated consciousness): a group that is wholly domesticated, without a spectrum of psyche or perceptual information related to consciousness itself.

They need to negate that their experience is domesticated, for they are after the fully formed aspect of consciousness. Additionally, they cannot admit that domestication is part of the process, for doing so would mean acknowledging that consciousness is not in its true form, but merely replicated or domesticated.

Thirdly, in admitting this, they would be on unstable ground, for they are neither domesticated in the sense of being separate from consciousness, nor are they consciousness-adjacent due to their domesticating process. This leaves them without a safe space when or if their process is questioned. They would be thrown into the depths of existential despair by losing access to any system; consciousness, because it was never truly accessed, and domestication, because they do not have an ideation of entering into such domestication. One needs a full experience of consciousness before embarking on the process of domestication.

As a result, they may find social interactions that involve forms of domestication uncomfortable, particularly when these forms seem "tamed" or controlled. This is because such interactions serve as a reminder of their own reality; being deeply embedded in domestication, despite their belief in having a conscious, independent experience. They might fail to recognize situations where something does not appear to be a domesticated process, although it actually is, because it aligns with the behavior of others who are also navigating this domesticated state of awareness.

They may not notice cases of actual domestication if it aligns with their counterpart's actions in domesticating consciousness.

At times, they might restructure their counterpart as a non-domesticated entity when there is a certain agreement in their manner of experience. Despite the appearance of what seems like a real domesticated process, the shared ideas may be enough for them to be convinced that the experience is non-domesticated. This is more often the case because domesticating consciousness still follows the process of consciousness, similar to how regular domestication operates; though it is a procedure of separation. With the content being somewhat the same, even if the approach differs, it is convincing enough to seem like a non-domesticated entry.

It is only when it becomes impossible to convince the psyche that the process is non-domesticated that they have no choice but to resort to other means. This typically happens when, even if the domesticated themes align with their process of domesticating consciousness, there is no way to attribute such occurrences as non-domesticated.

This situation may occur in the context of family, where it's difficult to convince the psyche to accept its own domesticated behavior due to overwhelming contradictory evidence. Similarly, in the case of public recognition, the domesticated aspect may align so closely with the consciousness they embrace that they cannot extricate it as non-domesticated. This is especially true with public distinction because they feel compelled to conform to public sentiment. Despite this, they struggle to accept that a domesticated process could reflect their true nature, which is deeply embedded within the domesticated system.

When there is no way to convince oneself that the process is non-domesticated, it leads to detestation, for they cannot accept the domesticated systems. Accepting this fact would denounce their entire enterprise as a paradox of domestication and consciousness. This often occurs when there is disagreement with the content they have domesticated; content that cannot be recalibrated as non-domesticated because they have not endured that process during the domestication of consciousness; hence, it must emanate from a domesticated realm.

In some ways, this is a fallacy based on a fallacy. In regular domestication, one could view consciousness from an almost infinite vantage point, where disagreement is inevitable. But since they are domesticating consciousness, they lack the ability to view consciousness from a perspective on consciousness itself. Instead, they view it as consciousness as a whole. When they do encounter a contrarian opinion, they must attribute it to domesticity because it cannot be non-domesticated. They have already undergone all of consciousness, and if there is disagreement, it must not partake in consciousness. Thus, the only choice is to categorize it as domesticated.

Secondly, there is the case where one carries robust domesticated themes that can only be attributed to a domesticated process and cannot be recalibrated as a non-domesticated one. Such themes include incoherence with direct sociality, mannerisms, procedures that disregard public experience or societal norms; anything that indicates a clear disenfranchisement from regular experiences within consciousness.

For example, picking one's nose, which is an act of disenfranchisement from society but still adheres to an internal system (as one engages in such an act while absorbed in internal rumination); must be attributed to domestication and cannot be classified as non-domestication.

This example is pertinent because there are cases where behaviors like defecating in public or other irregular, antisocial actions might be attributed to a dysfunction in personhood rather than being specifically domesticated. It is only when it is clear that domestication and non-domestication are contrasted with an understanding of which domain the behavior leans toward that such categorization becomes conceivable.

We'll often find that domestication is viewed as deflating the entire process, once it is acknowledged as such, by framing it as a fabrication of personhood, akin to antisocial behavior. This is because, by definition, it is antisocial to be disenfranchised from society. So even when one must admit to experiencing domestication, they might interpret it instead as another form of antisocial behavior, a dysfunction of personhood or an irregularity of mind; rather than a coherent domesticated process meant to contrast societal norms.

However, in the case of the example we have discussed, if it is clear that the domesticated process is not a dysfunction of personhood or antisocial behavior, but instead arises from individualized, internalized rumination; then even the attribution of antisocial behavior becomes a stretch for the psyche. In this case, one must admit that they are facing a domesticated individual; one who is enduring the true form of d-consciousness. It is the mannerisms that have a domesticated theme, such as picking one's nose, while also reflecting disenfranchisement from society's norms that demonstrate this process.

Another example would be an exaggerated excitement over simple infrastructure, which can only be understood as a withdrawal from the usual domesticated experience; a situation where such excitement is felt in its unadulterated form. Only individuals who come from a domesticated context would feel amusement or excitement over ordinary infrastructural elements. If they were in a non-domesticated state, they would not experience that same level of enthusiasm. Therefore, this reaction must be seen as a reflection of a domesticated mindset.

The only way to deal with apparent domestication is to perceive it as completely disingenuous. By discrediting the domesticated process, they can view their social counterpart as a fragmented version of their own process. In doing so, they retain their experience of d-consciousness despite its domesticated elements, which are not agreed upon as part of the equation.

When they can no longer dismiss domestication, they must enter a domain where they perceive full enmity toward the individual; as if that person is an abomination of existence itself. The opposing party is seen as a disruptive force that threatens their existential state, representing a breakdown of reality. It is never questioned that they might be following a disruptive formation of reality. Instead, they perceive their counterpart, who follows a normal formation, as highlighting the disruption. However, they reverse this perception to preserve their own identity. Hence, anything that opposes them is considered an abomination; a disruption of existence attributed to a domesticated process, which must be eradicated through various methods.

They are viewed not only as antisocial, merely a dysfunctional persona; but as individuals who have entered a state that signifies the breakdown of society itself. For them, society is understood as their version of a domesticated conscience, not society in its innate existence. They seem to facilitate the protection of society by entering into an insufferable relationship, acting on its behalf to remove those who threaten to break it apart. They perceive domestication, as a tool, not as one that supports society's growth, but as one that leads to its collapse.

There is enough evidence on their side because, at least in its embryonic state, domestication is a dissociation from society as a reanimated entity. But that is not its final purpose. Its aim is to engage the child through amusement, which in turn animates infrastructure and ensures its vitality in succession. If everyone turns away from its development, society will no longer function and will have to rely on the parasocial endowment provided by those who followed the domesticated process.

III.4 Infrastructure and the Urban Psyche

Another interesting phenomenon occurs: they disjoint from the very experience of direct access to consciousness, which is most prevalent in cities. Despite the possibility; none of which is less important than the domestication of consciousness; they reject this direct access. This is because interacting with consciousness, as such, requires a debated action within their criteria for interaction. As one person noted about cities, "there is no uniformity, each house has its own façade even when adjacent or connected"; which reminds them of dysfunction: what is connected, yet still unable to be different in its façade.

This observation highlights the core issue for those who domesticate consciousness: they find individuation within the city, intended to be a conscious haven. They struggle to reconcile the idea that an all-encompassing consciousness has manifested in a pattern of differentiation, leading them to believe that the very premise of consciousness within the city is disingenuous. They are reflecting on their own state, in which they cannot accept that they possess an individualized experience of consciousness. As a result, when they do encounter individuation, their initial response is one of apprehension.

Despite the fact that their experience of consciousness is rooted in their connection to the city's infrastructure, they cannot admit to the domesticated nature of the entire premise of consciousness. Therefore, they must assert that this infrastructure is inauthentic to the true form of consciousness. There is some truth to this claim, raw consciousness is all-encompassing; but the reflection is false. What they are truly reflecting upon is their domesticated state, which is a necessary condition for accessing consciousness, or at least its experiential aspect.

If we were to ask them, "Where do you find a true form of consciousness, if not through this disingenuous state of society?They would first assert that it lies in whatever surrounds them in their locality. They would further claim that they themselves embody the truth of consciousness. If pressed, they might even agree that they are, in fact, consciousness itself, which, of course, is a troubling assertion.

There is truth in their claim, however. In some theoretical sense, everything can be seen as consciousness, so it's not entirely unfounded to claim oneself as an all-encompassing consciousness. The issue lies in the nature of their experience and the process by which they arrive at this understanding. The manner in which they access this concept is through domesticated means, despite any theoretical framework to the contrary. This is why theoretical frameworks, in their raw state, are not practical: they have not been integrated into social reality and remain abstract. One does not experience themselves abstractly, nor do they follow an abstract procedure. Theory is simply a tool of the psyche, not an experiential state.

Moreover, the manner others perceive consciousness adds a layer complexity. The diversity of individuals within the city's infrastructure makes it impossible to attribute all of them to a specific lineage of consciousness. Instead, they must be understood as fragments of a particular domesticated sphere.

These individuals do not want direct access to consciousness because of the connotative data that comes along with it. Such access would challenge their premise and reveal the all-encompassing nature of consciousness, which does not conform to the individualized experiences they cling to. One need not look far in the city to observe its inherent differentiation; it's already understood to be more complex than mere individuation. Thus, it is preferable to domesticate consciousness from a vantage point that has some access to prevailing data, but without the realization or experience of individuation.

This creates a quandary for them. Without certain access, they risk domestication of an imaginative form of consciousness, which undermines the integrity of their entire approach. The society they must engage to gain access will be limited; filled with projections of what it might have been to experience consciousness directly.

This is a critical observation: not only do they fail to retain consciousness from its real-time source, but they also avoid the very premise of it. Instead, they rely on a former memory as a bookmark, integrating it with a limited version of society; one distant enough from true consciousness to allow continued participation without dissatisfaction. The result is an admixture of a former ideal and a suboptimal current reality.

III.5 Involuntary Domestication

Involuntary domestication occurs when a system of consciousness pervades the infrastructure, requiring individuals to participate in that representation to give the system recognition. When this participation is not forthcoming, the imposed agenda of domestication takes a form that may appear innocent, but in fact this unadulterated form is a different kind of structure. We can begin with an example: consider the domesticated thought, "I am annoyed right now." It is domesticated because the reason for this feeling, aside from the internal workings of the system, remains unclear; like the gears of an engine or the behind-the-scenes components of any complex system.

Just as the hidden elements of a system are experienced as a shadow, they represent matters that have reached the point of appearance but are not yet ready to be solely revealed. These elements are situated in the background, unable to predict their final destination; much like the engine's gears, which do not exhibit as the vehicle itself but are nonetheless essential. However, being essential, these elements have no social utility when shown publicly, as they become a denial of the liminal parts that constitute the final system. The same can be said of the body: its internal organs, though essential to its function, are invisible to the social sphere. They are the body's "shadow," for they cannot display affection themselves but provide the foundation for the final expression of affection we call the "wholesome individual."

Similarly, domestication works in the same way. Take the thought "I am annoyed right now." It is a pernicious thought, but one that would not be displayed to the social sphere. It reflects an internal state, which contributes to the overall social experience, but it does not elicit affection on its own. It is "abdominal," not because it is untrue, but because it is only a partial truth, entrenched too deeply to communicate implicitly within or outside the system.

The thought "I am annoyed" offers little in terms of inner communication. It is an axiomatic interjection that can only be met with responses like, "No, you are not," or "Why are you annoyed?" This is an opening for further communication to build a more complete picture of the situation. For example, "No, you are not" could evolve into "Yes, you are because of X," and further into "What is the cause of X?" Through this process, we build a fuller comprehension of the sentiment; not because of the annoyance itself but because of the context in which it arises, which can then be responded in numerous ways.

The domesticated sentiment is so deeply entrenched that it allows little availability for dynamic interaction. It serves no purpose other than to be extrapolated into potential social communication. Whereas it is part of the psyche, it isolates the individual, making it difficult for the mind and social environment to exchange significant communication.

If communicated at such a complex level, whether for the sake of the psyche or the social sphere, the sentiment becomes a burden for both. For the psyche, copiously accepting this sentiment without adaptation would make it the dominant force, causing all other thoughts to give precedence to that one. This leads to a social manifestation, where the belief in the sentiment as truth, within the perceptual sphere, reinforces the idea that the annoyance has both a cause and direction, while leaving no availability for change within the psyche. In turn, social communication becomes burdened since it cannot be questioned; it is axiomatic and only serves to validate the sentiment, thereby strengthening its perceived truth.

Additionally, the causative effect is that social communication would require others to accept that sentiment as if it were their own. Soon, many individuals may find themselves experiencing the same annoyance; simply because one person introduced a domesticated thought into the social sphere, which was then accepted and spread as the axiomatic sentiment of society. Like a virus, it finds countless reasons to validate its sentiment; there is no shortage of such reasons in the human experience. However, these reasons are merely attached to the sentiment, which was already accepted as axiomatic. Naturally, this will cease at some point, as not everyone will agree with the sentiment. Some may choose to either confront their inner state or challenge the sentiment itself.

This is why we consider involuntary domestication as one of the factors creating a social shadow: the discord between regular social affairs and an individual's distress generates a natural context in which they are seen as inferior and complacent. This cannot be controlled. One must either accept their sentiment or view them as demoralized, unleashing their inner turmoil without the means to communicate within the broader, more general system.

Due to this dynamic, involuntary domestication seeks elements of society that are sentimental and relevant, applying these elements to their domestication. They do not wish to remain mere shadows, so they inject ideas that are of strong interest to the social system. For example, one might adopt an annoyance as an axiomatic sentiment and then introduce issues like relationship struggles; topics that, in any society, are often compelling. Even if they are not personally contending with these complexities, they understand that such subjects will captivate the surrounding environment. With this enticement, the onlooker is coerced into accepting the validity of relationship issues as a true sentiment; transforming the individual from a demoralized figure into one who represents broader societal dynamics.

The only way out of this predicament is through a controlled context, in which the individual is recognized as the shadow they embody: a person in distress, but with the understanding that this sentiment is part of a broader lineage of representation; true yet incomplete. It is true that relationship woes are personal matters, but they do not represent the entire representation. If we are drawn to vulnerability, it follows that the system causing that vulnerability has the right to bear it, making it valuable as part of a greater, more wholesome process.

III.6 Fixation vs. Domestication Consciousness

Fixation differs from d-consciousness in a very real way. While fixation is existential, domestication is contrary in its contrivance. Fixation, such as seen in a workaholic, attends to the task at hand without repose, attenuating selfhood to become the fabric of the work system. Domesticating that very workforce, on the other hand, would align selfhood to be more inclined toward the workplace.

The differentiation becomes pronounced in the mediator between selfhood and the object of inquiry. Fixation operates without a mediator, as one can remain fixated on the same object throughout maturity. In contrast, d-consciousness involves a mechanism of the psyche that intermediates between the object of inquiry and selfhood. Thus, we have the term alignment for the latter, and becoming for the former; workplace for the latter, and work-system for the former.

The reason we associate the workplace with d-consciousness is that the focus of the object is the constitution of the work environment, and consciousness is attached solely to property and its subsidiaries. The notion of a work system or work environment, on the other hand, refers to an existential attachment in which the object of fixation is a contrived view of what requires activity for upholding the constitution. This view opposes the principles or sentiments of the workplace, following only the precepts that lead to the creation of the work environment. Following this definition, a workaholic can never be considered for domestication of consciousness. Fixation forms an existential makeup from which domestication follows, not the other way around.

Domestication, in this respect, is the familiarity that arises from a constitution or existential reality. As long as one attaches to a constitution in a more pathological manner, they will experience that domestication. Consider a political representative, a judge, for instance. They are unavailable to the enjoyment of their domesticated parts as their role in law but rather attach themselves to the experience of being a judge. Thus, they are becoming a judge, not aligning with it.

On the other hand, one does not become their family body but builds, supports, aligns with, or chooses their family; actions that exemplify domestication. If one were to say, "I am becoming family" as a noun, or that they are their family to the exclusion of all else, not that nothing else matters, but rather that existence itself is defined solely by family; then we can suspect that it is a fixation rather than a process of domestication.

One can domesticate consciousness only when there is either a constitution or context to access consciousness itself. Constitutions of state represent consciousness both with and without deference to that state, serving as portals to consciousness, closely tied to its fabric. A constitution can be made in any locality as long as there is a reference to material property and a social agreement. One cannot brand a constitution for themselves in regards themselves, for they are the constitution to which they attend. In other words, a constitution is the creation of personhood outside of personhood, such that anything directly linking to personhood would not be considered part of the constitution.

A dystopian workplace, political reality, or social group are all forms of d-consciousness because there is a constitution, reaching a state of dystopian when sociality openly domesticates its contents without mediation. Although we previously noted that d-consciousness involves mediation, it is theoretically possible to domesticate consciousness without it.

In this case, a lean ego is tasked with mediation, and without it, fixation would result. With just a fragment of self-reference, one can domesticate consciousness without a formative ego structure or other contexts. This results in a dystopian state because the ego is subjugated but not expelled; subordinated enough to filter a domesticated channel that links directly to the consciousness sentiment. Thus, they embody the state rather than understand or become exceedingly fixated upon it.

We term such 'dystopian' because we assume it to be a negative outcome of a political system or social structure, where the individual essentially subjugates themselves by reframing their familiar aspects to align with the state.

The availability of d-consciousness is made possible only when two things are adjacent: adherence to the principles and/or constitution, and the maintenance of domesticated elements and/or relatability to that system. This explains why an individual may become excessively infatuated with political representatives, perceiving them as akin to family members. This allows the familial aspect (or domestic element) to become attached to the constitution. However, the mediator must be tamed so as not to intrude and engage in intellectual discourse, as this would create further separation. There must be alignment that ensures one remains contextually confined, away from the direct impact of the consciousness reception.

Since consciousness is a regular stream despite concerning social structures, the more competent the structure, the more tenable consciousness will be. Although we assume the political entity to be the highest threshold, it becomes relatively minuscule in contrast to the infrastructure itself, allowing one to domesticate consciousness from infrastructure. When consciousness is directly linked to genuine experience, one becomes existentially confined to an abridged version of consciousness. These typically go together because when there is political exertion, it usually coincides with infrastructure. This is why the capitals of competent states are removed from the nexus of their civilizations, they avoid becoming mixed.

The lower one goes on the spectrum of possible consciousness, the less complicated the d-consciousness becomes. In an interactive domain that already has a structure designed to prevent direct attachment to consciousness, the domestication process becomes more benign. For example, some family structures might lead a child to domesticate the entire consciousness experience within that family. However, if the child detaches at some point, without prolonged engagement, the harm tends to be minimal.

However, if there is either a prolonged period in the low form or excessive vitality in the high form of consciousness, the consequences will be more detrimental. One will have conditioned their systems to the domesticated process, resulting in an unsafe existential separation. In this state, an analyst could extract the unconscious, and the merger between the two would happen instantly. In such a case, one would become regularly attached to what is personal to them and would no longer possess the tools or capacity to perceive differently.

For example, in serious cults, there is little possibility of assistance, even through psychology, because their entire system of relatability has been reconstructed according to the consciousness of the cult. While we can eventually restore their previous relational structure, this requires navigating an intricate web of constructs; much like an actor fully embodying their character. This process involves extracting the subconscious attachments between the art form and the psyche. The prolonged attachment means that a complete analysis of the structure must take place before we can rebuild something that correlates to the personality prior to the exposure, allowing the two parts of the psyche to interact once more.

In the case of d-consciousness shaped by infrastructure and encapsulated in high form, a complete breakdown of the psyche occurs, allowing a new form of consciousness to filter through the channels. Instead of being ruled by the usual gatekeepers of relatability and context at each interval, the psyche stumbles through like a drunk person unaware of social discord. The psyche cannot resist this course until it settles, at which point one faces a crucial choice: either to reframe that consciousness with a contextual overlay or to continue abiding by the domesticated form of consciousness.

III.7 THE LIMITS OF DOMESTICATION AND ITS DISCONTENTS

Domesticated content cannot be recognized as domesticated. We can only domesticate content once; any attempt at further domestication proves futile. As discussed in earlier works, a domesticated process that follows another domestication resembles corporate or work structures. It merely creates the illusion of internalizing reality, without truly engaging with it.

A noteworthy conclusion many religions reach is that they offer a domestication of content where the family dynamic further perpetuates this domestication. Here, because the religion itself is a domestication of content, further emphasis on domestication within the family structure leads to a fabricated and projected dynamic. How, then, can individuals engage in an existential exchange about contexts that pertain not to reality itself, but to a domesticated version of it?

We are not critiquing religious doctrine or any other structure where contextual frameworks are domesticated. This process provides access to a vast assortment of information that would not exist otherwise. The domestication of content functions similarly to the way corporations represent economic and social structures: it offers a framework through which individuals can understand reality, not as it truly is, but as a superficial structure. It is a traditional, ancient, or otherwise structured doctrine that repeats aspects in a redundant format. However, in engaging with this structure, individuals gain a nuanced understanding of reality that would remain inaccessible without this domestication.

One might counter the claim that external content is domesticated by noting that the family body provides a regular, concurrent domestication of all external exposure. However, the family body does not maintain the strict parameters of a defined formula for perception. The domestication of certain content, bound by strict parameters, provides something the family body cannot.

In a broader sense, we could say that academic fields are domestications of external experience. They offer contextual frameworks that allow us to perceive the rest of reality. However, academic fields are usually not intended to uncover nuances beyond their boundaries. They adhere strictly to their own parameters and understanding. Fields like psychology, sociology, and other socially adaptable research do serve to uncover deeper nuances of reality. Yet, they do not provide the kind of domestication or traditional parameters that remain static. These fields are dynamic and evolve with time, which means they do not offer a stable foundation for perceiving the external world. Traditional frameworks, on the other hand, retain their redundancy, offering stability that allows for continuous reflection upon reality.

In this sense, academic fields can be used not for their material structure or development, but for their immovable nature; despite being disputed or illogical. They serve as reference points for existential awareness. For example, in psychology, the works of Freud, Bauer, and others may not represent the cutting edge of the field, but they remain valuable for gaining perspective on reality, despite their lack of logical consistency. The absence of continued logical progression does not invalidate a logical system; it merely means that the system no longer serves the scientific goals of modern inquiry.

Ultimately, the process of domestication, whether through rigid traditional frameworks or evolving academic ones; proves ineffective when applied to real-life dynamics, such as within the family or social group structures. One might imagine a mathematician who struggles to domesticate or socially exchange about their mathematical endeavors. The true dynamics of domestication concern the lived experience of reality, and because externality does not resonate with mathematical abstraction, it will not become an existential interest of sociality. While another individual may remain attached to this context of inquiry, that attachment does not constitute domestication. It is simply the engagement of agents providing nuance through research, akin to the imaginary discussions one might have when digesting thought material.

III.8 Domestication of Consciousness: Familiarity, Fragmentation, and the Limits of Psyche

It can be presumed that domestication is a process of becoming familiar with the already experienced elements of consciousness. Without a pre-existing encapsulation of consciousness, it would be challenging to assume that one can fully comprehend or familiarize themselves with the reality framework they have attenuated.

Given the nature of higher life forms and the multiple frames of consciousness already available; regardless of the circumstances, if one overlays domestication, they may become familiar with every possibility contained by their psyche. They could achieve a complete domestication of even the most extreme aspects of their conscious experience. However, with the overextension of domestication, they risk losing touch with the deeper processes of the psyche. In more typical cases, they might begin to actualize the domesticated content in such a way that it no longer feels familiar to the psyche. Instead, it manifests as a new format that extends the psyche; even though, at first glance, it may still appear to be domesticated material.

We will begin by considering the rare situation where one continuously domesticates to the point where the entire psyche becomes dependent on a particular form of consciousness sentiment, leaving no space for alternative perspectives. In this scenario, the individual becomes overly familiar with their own process, rendering it impossible to transcend it. They have utilized all available vitality in the act of domestication, thereby limiting their capacity to reconnect with the raw consciousness from which they once derived attention and agency. This phenomenon is often observed when individuals begin to regularly dissociate or lose focus on reality, as they have domesticated their awareness to such an extent that they struggle to reestablish conscious attention.

Intellectuality itself functions as a form of domestication, driven by the primary motivation to detail and expand upon an encapsulation of consciousness to its furthest depths. The goal is not so much to become familiar with it, but to compartmentalize it; breaking apart the holistic nature of consciousness into distinct segments. Consequently, a singular, unified house becomes a row of houses, simplifying the process of domestication. Even within this intellectual framework, domestication remains necessary because all one accomplishes is the compartmentalization of an already conscious experience, without ever beginning the process of truly engaging with, or becoming familiar with, the contents of these compartments.

III.9 DOMESTICATION OF CONSCIOUSNESS: MONEY, POLITICS, AND THE EROSION OF THE SELF

The domestication of consciousness is the process by which raw, unmediated social awareness is structured and controlled by social frameworks. This is not merely an individual transformation but a systemic phenomenon, where consciousness is not engaged directly but instead filtered through highly noticeable manifestations of infrastructure; most notably, money and politics. As a result, the most politically applicable elements of consciousness become the only material deemed relevant at all, as they are the easiest to quantify and integrate into the broader social system. Money, as a necessary factor in all workforce structures, ultimately becomes the only factor. In a domesticated system, consciousness is assumed to be directly structured through these tangible, simplified layers.

A child will learn that the world operates on finance, not as a secondary fact but as the foundational truth of their reality. This is not a complex idea; rather, it is the most accessible way to approach consciousness when its depth and multiplicity have already been domesticated into simplistic, political manifestations. Instead of perceiving the workforce as a dynamic interaction of various intellectual and creative forces, finance becomes the single defining aspect, and every other factor is absorbed into this framework. Consciousness is reduced to a political and economic metric, one that is universally tangible, measurable, and, most importantly, domesticated.

The most noticeable detriment of this system is that it leaves individuals without any independent means of self-definition. When every level of one's organization is built upon political and economic structures, any disruption to these structures results in a forfeiture of selfhood. If money declines, the individual loses their intrinsic esteem. If political structures falter, the same collapse occurs. In such a scenario, the only available recourse is violence, either toward self or others, as an attempt to recover from this systemic decline.

This occurs because the domestication of consciousness does not merely regulate external behaviors; it restructures the psyche itself. If an individual has no ability to interact separate from the frameworks imposed upon them, any loss within those frameworks is experienced as a total failure of existence. Without access to the raw, unmediated forms of consciousness that existed prior to domestication, there is no alternative space from which to rebuild or redefine one's identity. The result is a system that not only confines consciousness to a domesticated form but also ensures that individuals are unable to function outside of it.

This creates a cycle where consciousness is increasingly reduced to the most quantifiable and socially ingrained forms. Money and politics do not just dominate the workforce and public life, they become the exclusive channels through which consciousness is expressed and understood. A society that measures everything through political or economic value inevitably dismisses all other forms of human experience. As d-consciousness deepens, the range of potential interactions narrows, ensuring the system remains self-perpetuating. The individual, now fully immersed in a world where only money and politics matter, cannot imagine life beyond these constraints.

This results in a society where selfhood is defined solely by economic standing and political involvement. When either of these fails, individuals are left unable to comprehend their existence, often turning to self-destruction or violence as perceived solutions. The system, having d-consciousness to this extent, ensures that even in crisis, individuals remain ensnared within the frameworks it has imposed.

Politics follows the same trajectory. If we construct a system where political engagement is embedded into every level of an individual's organization, then politics itself becomes the only recognized form of conscious participation. This means that only political realities which are easily tangible at every level of sophistication will emerge, as they are the most efficiently domesticated. Politics, rather than being a space for genuine interaction with complexity, becomes a pre-packaged, easily consumed framework through which people understand their own agency.

One does not merely "engage" in politics; rather, one becomes a political agent by virtue of existing within this framework. Politics and the individual become intertwined, rendering them indistinguishable. As political climates evolve, so too does the individual's sense of self, as there is no distinct boundary between their consciousness and the political reality they occupy. When political structures falter, the individual experiences this as a direct personal crisis. Similarly, just as economic decline dictates self-worth through the lens of money, political collapse manifests as a crisis of identity, with no clear separation between the individual and the political system.

III.10 THE LIMITS OF AMBITION

There is another aspect of the domestication of consciousness: a clearer understanding of commitment, as distinct from ambition. Ambition can be defined as an existential attachment to a specific objective, while commitment involves accepting the broader criteria that make that objective possible. Though these two traits may appear similar, they are as distinct as different species. Commitment is not merely about adapting to enter all the gateways leading to the final objective, but about embracing the expansive and unrelenting parameters that enable accountability and proportion within a larger framework. In this sense, commitment is the maintenance of awareness toward the objective, rather than a fixation on achieving it directly.

In contrast, ambition disregards everything except the end goal. When someone becomes overly ambitious, they become beholden to the objective without recognizing or engaging with the components that make it achievable. They fail to evaluate the structure of the objective as they pursue it.

In the context of domestication of consciousness; where one is consistently reflecting on consciousness itself without regard for its context; it cannot be framed as ambition toward consciousness. That would overlook the need for commitment to the structure of consciousness and to one's individuality comprised by it.

Typically, one must commit to elements, aspects, and environments that are not immediately accessible or appealing in their raw form. While one might seek relief from this inaccessibility, they continue to assertively maintain the goal. If the objective were clearly delineated, however, commitment would not be required, interaction itself would be unnecessary.

Thus, commitment becomes essential when the conscious substance at the heart of the objective is complex or disruptive. What we often overlook is that all conscious substance is inherently disruptive and formatted, and therefore requires a form of commitment that provides a constant stream of context from various angles. This ensures that one does not develop at the mercy of the raw substance itself. The reason we associate commitment with the more challenging aspects of life, work, or other endeavors is that it is precisely in these areas where the highest amounts of conscious substance are offered. It is challenging because many elements serve as a buffer, shielding from direct interaction with consciousness, thus preventing a dearth in awareness of its contextual bridge or of the individuality within it.

We may assume that there are "gatekeepers" of consciousness, but in reality, these are necessary elements that provide context. These mediating factors may take the form of people or nature. When we encounter a loss of tangibility in conscious substance; whether due to some alluring aspect of ourselves or because the substance seems to promise a consciousness that is ultimately absent; commitment becomes necessary. In the latter case, the goal is not to gain further access to the conscious substance, but rather to provide distance. This ensures that the appearance of conscious substance does not mislead us, and prevents us from becoming existentially entangled in that domain.

For example, maturity requires accepting the hygiene of using a restroom. This is a childhood milestone and one of its significant modifications, in which one finds commitment, not ambition; in this domain. If a child entertains the notion of ambition; attempting to become existentially attached to the restroom process and perfect it, they will only find the opposite: it becomes the most burdensome of daily routines because it has not been committed in its proper form.

This is not to say that there is no underlying conscious substance associated with the restroom process; though there is much to discuss in that regard, according to Freud; but for our purposes, it is assumed to have a weak conscious approval. The reason commitment is necessary is precisely because of this faint conscious substance, yet it is an area one must engage in as part of their daily routine. Without commitment, one becomes existentially attached. By the mere fact of entering that domain every day, one either falls into natural ambition or learns the commitment required to accept its process, despite its faintness of consciousness.

Thus, the most successful restroom procedure is one in which a person commits and distances themselves from it as a source of conscious substance. Instead, they see it as a process requiring attention, despite its limited effect on overall development. It is commitment despite its weakness. Once commitment is made, one accepts the process without existential engagement, recognizing it as a simple procedure that must be followed from start to finish, without having significant impact on the psyche or human endeavors.

The same can be said for sleep, toward which nobody exhibits ambition. Anyone who tries to approach sleep with ambition finds the opposite: the psyche constantly seeks out the notion of sleep, intertwining itself with the idea and ultimately losing individuality and the sense of a final objective. The proper approach is to commit to sleep, thereby providing context and creating a bridge between two waking states, which would otherwise go unrecognized in the experience of life.

One might argue that there is conscious substance in both sleep and the restroom procedure, but it cannot be accessed directly. Instead, it requires a complex framework of context, and the most straightforward approach is commitment. When one commits, they contextualize the entire experience, making it a sideline to regular psyche interaction, thereby forfeiting its energy consumption and time allocation.

Commitment differs from context. While context provides comprehension within a specific realm, commitment is the acceptance of the entire structure, including its implications and underlying factors; as a contextual bridge. When one commits to something, they accept whatever it entails, and whatever its costs; across multiple frameworks. This commitment is rooted in a specific context, but it does not need to be elaborated; it may be the commitment to an unsubstantiated idea, for example.

Context, on the other hand, cannot be insubstantial. It must be a mechanism to provide nuance within a specific realm, without regard for the broader domain. It grants access to certain components, not as an acceptance of its overall themes, but as the creation of a smaller domain within a larger one. While one must accept this context and enter the domain for a particular purpose, they will only see things through that lens.

However, without a prior commitment to the larger sphere of that realm, a specific domain-like context cannot progress. How could one create a domain-like context within a larger, overarching domain that pertains not only to that specific context, but also to overall psyche function? First, one must accept and engage with the domain as it exists, before entering a context shaped by that domain.

One might think they can simply create a context and interact with raw consciousness through the lens of that context, but without a specifically structured and concrete domain to mediate that interaction, they become detached from the infrastructure that supports that conscious element.

For example, one cannot browse areas of high levels of consciousness, assuming they have the proper context through which to interact and gain access to raw conscious substance; not by direct interaction, but through that contextual layer. If they stray from or bypass the domain-like elements embedded in the infrastructure that allow for that specific direction of consciousness, they lose access.

Thus, the only way context can serve as a gateway to consciousness is through, first and foremost, a concrete acceptance and commitment to its domain. This ensures that one does not become privy to the entire nature of the psyche or overall consciousness, but instead allows for the creation of a contextual layer that serves as a doorway.

III.11 THE POSTURE OF DOMESTICATED CONSCIOUSNESS

There is no possible dialogue or didactic inference to postured d-consciousness. The entire informational repertoire of one who has d-consciousness is not in sync with the informational elements themselves, which makes for availability and dialogue, but rather is elements of a piece of reality that they have brought to bear, all contained by their psyche.

These are not simple ideas nor knowledge for the psyche, but rather are in themselves the formation of reality with no other reality available with no other aspect of the psyche ready for a negotiation of that reality. It is simply the posture of an exemplified reality, as though the infrastructure itself is speaking and saying: this is real as an object and is infrastructure itself, one which cannot be argued with. The reason that one becomes performative in their d-consciousness realm is because there is a sentiment by which they feel disappointed with compulsory reality by virtue of meeting a social counterpart of natural differentiation; as though simply showing up to the dialogue without a word of exchange is already a form of contestation; as the reality framework is in question by mere proximity of social differentiation.

However, the information that happens to permeate their psyche is by no means unsubstantiated; rather, there are tidbits of a true form of reality that has no sequence with each other or with broader reality, but rather are tidbits of genuine information. We could thus state the clause that anyone with d-consciousness who postures information will proclaim pieces of knowledge that are true forms of infrastructural reality and are necessary components of any social discourse. This differs from the possibility of having knowledge or information that has no basis in current reality or in any reality, and d-consciousness is true to its nature as only being based upon reality as it is.

This does not mean that it is sequenced or synchronized with any of its pieces of information or with what is more broad than it, but only that each piece of information is true and must be recognized as true. That does not mean that one can interact with a persona of d-consciousness, since they have postured a synchronicity and sequence that is not only false in its premise but has no basis of logical lineage. Even if one wishes to interact, they would be interacting with something that is true in its elements but is constantly weaving new sequences to make it appear logical as a composite reality. In its composite nature there is no ability for interaction, because, first, the individual is posturing reality, not information, and secondly, the sequence that they have proposed based on the tidbits of information has no logical bearing and does not substantiate itself upon a formation that is available for dynamic discourse.

The only method of interacting with d-consciousness is by extracting the tidbits of information, as it is known to be completely genuine; meaning to say that they are unpredictable strobes of light that all contain actuality in themselves but have no verity in their sequence between each other. And in this way one can provide their own sequence away from the d-consciousness realm, which can extract and understand those pieces of information in an interactive manner such that they are not attempting to acquiesce to all of reality but only to the contextual footing of whatever they are in pursuit of.

Thus, to deal with d-consciousness is to not interact with it, for in any interaction one will begin to posture their own version of reality, since the psyche recognizes that they are in opposition to one who claims all of reality, and in such cases will then attempt to proclaim another form of reality that is alternative to it, but more so that proves they are existent within the claimed reality which appears to disregard their entire form of existence. Meaning to say, even if one is not in a state of d-consciousness, by simply interacting with d-consciousness they will posture an alternative reality in order to proceed and claim their right of existence, which is constantly being diminished by the claim of the opposing party and their composite reality which does not include them.

Yet, with all this said and done, one cannot ignore the details that are postured from that form of d-consciousness, as they are enticing for the very reason that they are a form of genuine reality. Thus, one must also participate with their own interactive layer that provides a sequence not in the manner that it is being postured but rather based on their own criteria, by which they extract those tidbits of information in order to input a coherent logical mainframe. But this is only possible if one interacts from the vantage of being silent rather than directly interacting, for the reason that if such is done then they will begin to posture their own formation of reality. They do so from the silent vantage point to thus extract from a corrupted headline that surely has important information but is not possible to be in direct interaction with, but is also not possible to ignore because of its convergence with reality.

Case Study: Artificial Intelligence as Context

Artificial intelligence is a framework for approaching data that is both relevant and irrelevant to sociality. This can be compared to any database of knowledge, even if its genre is expansive. In dealing with such, we simply need to regard it as we would any database of knowledge, and, in that manner, continue to do so.

However, as with any framework of contextuality that broaches upon reality, it can be circumvented as a basis because of its innate distinction and separation from reality. Thus one can be d-consciousness, to which this form of context is now in service but has little dimension into reality and consciousness itself. Commonly, this does not occur with a regular library of knowledge because the mere act of participation in that domain—whether structurally (library) or materially (book or other form of medium)—serves to mediate between the realm of reality and that of context.

One who reads a fantasy and thus views reality as such will be considered socially inept, yet less so if the medium is film, and even less so if it is socially communicated as a serious approach to reality. Although regular social discourse is also based on individuals and their distinct contexts, because there is less appearance of the medium that proves it is context-based, it is more possible to conjure a reality framework that is believed to be reality itself.

One may inquire whether there is any reality, especially when noticing that, more often than not, there is a context underpinning a reality framework. In a way, that is true, although there is an objective reality that is foremost within nature. The context that approaches that reality offers access to that reality, which cannot be accessed separately from context because of its innate permeability and completeness. Any inquiry into artificial intelligence that treats it as more than a framework—either as an existential threat, as sentient, or in any comparable regard—is manifestly based on the belief that it has somehow surpassed being a context by virtue of not noticing the format of its medium.

In fact, the very inquiry into its existential possibility—whether against existent beings or for being existent in its own right—postures the notion that there is no context separating the individual from their interaction. More so, it may be the case that the very inquiry is what generates the entire enticement of the subject, as if there is an existential possibility such that one must at least entertain the notion that there is no context.

As with any knowledge database, it is either closely associated with current reality or less associated. Artificial intelligence is closely associated by virtue of its infrastructural tenacity toward every point of knowledge in addition to general social discourse. Secondarily, it loses its notation as a medium of context because it removes all barriers that might offer the impression of something separate from it—such as materiality or infrastructural manifestation—as well as the streamlined nature of falling directly into sync with normal sociality.

However, nothing has changed other than the loss of a distinction rather than its manifest process. The entire premise of paralleling it with other forms of reality—warranting existential questions or existential threats, or consciousness or lack thereof—is only possible when one assumes the experience of interacting with reality itself, but more so with d-consciousness, by applying infusion of data points that are surely participating in consciousness and directly domesticating its substance, all without noticing the context and/or domain between reality and that inference.

The question of whether a book is sentient is never asked, nor whether it can produce an existential threat—which surely it can—nor whether there is consciousness within it—which surely it can infer—because it is acknowledged as a medium to consciousness, very much because it is noticed as such. The only difference in the mode of knowledge is the lack of noticeability in its distinction, coupled with its alignment to its inference of consciousness. Any further discourse only reveals the process by which one has domesticated consciousness through that medium.

SECTION IV: THERAPEUTIC MENDING & INTERVENTIONS

IV.1 THERAPEUTIC MENDING IN INTERACTIVE DOMAINS

AUTHOR'S NOTATION:

This section does not directly explore the philosophical construct of domestication, but rather the internal process of domestication, specifically how domestication generates itself from within, whether contained by the psyche or within the social arena. Although we term this "therapeutic mending," it is merely the manner in which two elements of contrasting characteristics interact under the umbrella of domestication. It concerns how social adhesiveness reveals itself within the framework of domestication, which is most apparent on the personal level.

There are two categories of individuals who require therapeutic mending; perhaps no other categories exist: one who is engaged in a conscious continuum, and the other who is involved in an interactive structure. The second group, those involved in an interactive structure, require therapeutic mending despite the dominance of interactivity in claiming experience and shaping the psyche.

The Internal Logic of Interactive Domains

When there is a constant flow of interactivity, it seems that such a domain should provide an ongoing possibility of maintaining, regulating, and stabilizing one's interactive well-being. Instead, the opposite occurs. The interactive domain, focused on a specific context of interactivity, demands that the individual psyche project all its internal interactions in proportion to the prevailing sentiment.

However the psyche operates, it will only retract according to the interactive interests of the moment.

One might argue that an individual may be unable to recognize their personal experience within the interactivity of such a domain, as the experience becomes aligned with the social context. One will become more attuned to the changing sentiment of this sociality, leading to significant alterations in personal experience. This happens because personal interactive experiences are only accessible through the interactive domain.

The key idea is that any peripheral interactivity becomes vital to the psyche, leaving no room for competing interactive aspects, especially those of personal significance. The structure of interactive domains tends to integrate aspects of interactivity that may not align with the desired direction. Therefore, efforts will be made to regulate interaction through contextual constraints, ensuring that non-consequential interactivity does not impede more personal, potentially disruptive forms of interaction.

Non-Consequential Interactivity and Repression

Non-consequential interactivity is a core requirement of any interactive domain. When it becomes consequential, it loses its integrity as a distinct entity that participates in regular social cycles.[5] Thus, the very proclamation of being an interactive domain may be a mechanism for avoiding genuine interactivity, offering instead safe,

---

[5] Kaplan's theory aligns with some of these principles. Where we differentiate is the physical space that is asserted by them, especially in the need of nature. We can find results where nature can be fairly harmful as an interactive domain, rather becoming a habitat to degenerate the entire civilized process of the psyche that can have a broad ranging effects. Kaplan, S., & Kaplan, R. (1989). The Experience of Nature: A Psychological Perspective. Cambridge University Press.

non-consequential interactivity that lacks existential significance or real-world consequences.

If completed perfectly, therapeutic mending would not be necessary, as the interactivity animating the psyche would be irrelevant to initiating any interactive ensemble within it. In other words, due to its non-consequential nature, there would be no taxing personal interactive experience to address, as it is disallowed. To be fair, there would still be some demand for psyche interactivity, but repression would play a significant role in preventing the need for mending, as it assumes control.

In summary, the interactive domain does require therapeutic mending, but only insofar as it raises interactivity within the psyche through its processes. The nature of interactive domains is highly contextual, so the necessity for mending is less about concern for the domain itself and more about the disruption caused by inter-system interactivity. While such domains offer a haven from the vast scale of universal interactivity, they cannot shield their own internal structure. The engagement with the system inevitably draws attention to the line separating the domain from its parameters, becoming a focal point of contention and controversy.

Therapeutic mending is needed to repair the interactivity that arises from the very analogy of the interactive domain as inside universal reality. These elements create costly interactivity within the domain, so that one experiences aspects of their psyche's complex when they meet the domain's parameters. It is similar to a simulation: while the notion of being inside the simulation remains undisturbed, only upon its disassembly or violation of its parameters does the interactivity take on a nuanced, existential quality. The same is true for love or romance; the experience within the domain of love is not as interactive as its beginning or disintegration.

Therapeutic mending is required for love when it is threatened because, at that point, the interactive elements of love have existential weight, given that the domain of love cannot shield the connection. One could even argue that the disruption caused by the chaotic interactivity at the end of love has less to do with love itself, and more with one's relationship to their existential domain and further interactions. At this juncture, therapeutic mending is needed because the interactivity becomes highly volatile and no longer represents the amelioration of present interactive singularity, but rather shifts into unpredictable assumptions rooted in one's existential history.

The Sequence Problem: Irregularity and Temporal Disruption

Mending is required to mold all these interactive aspects into a cohesive whole, establishing a present interactive direction rather than an irregular, disjointed experience derived from the individual's entire history. When each interactive element is not sequentially aligned with another, each will rise to prominence and disrupt the others, with no clear hierarchy or sequence. While this may seem like a proper approach to irregular interactivity, embracing it as the experience of the psyche; we fail to honor the truth of each element as it exists in itself.

When we focus on a single irregular interactive element, we notice it has a complex basis, shaped by a specific measure of consciousness. As though the rumination of consciousness permeates life, each interactive moment encapsulates a single measure of that rumination. The allegiance of that interactive moment is to the conscious continuum, so irregular interactivity becomes multiple quantities of consciousness that are not sequentially aligned, each seeming to dominate the others in turn. If we were to revisit the moment where this interactivity was first experienced, it would have occurred in sequence through the underlying psyche and consciousness. But now, even if it regains vitality, the interactivity no longer follows the correct order.

To restore these elements to sequence, therapeutic mending can take place, affecting the entire interactive landscape and integrating it into a cohesive whole. This process would create a single interactive encapsulation, including, but not limited to, the present moment. With mending in place, the natural sequence would take over, so that irregular demands of interactivity are integrated according to their relative importance within the system.

Natural vs. Conscious Mending

This process occurs naturally when one is in a situation devoid of irregular interactivity. In the case of love, while contained by the experience, the interactivity is naturally resolved to incorporate all demands, thus bringing them into the present stage. This happens without conscious effort. The simple state of being enamored with the domain causes the interactivity of the moment to become prominent enough to absorb all interactive demands. However, when one transitions into irregular interactivity, it becomes a conscious effort to manage the interaction and mold into a single, coherent present, so that prior interactive elements do not disrupt the current system.

There are reasons why some moments of therapeutic mending happen naturally, while others require conscious effort:

Level of Interactive Exposure: As seen in love or any interactive domain, the interactivity present is relatively limited, with nothing in the current moment pulling from the entire landscape of one's existential vulnerabilities. Therefore, in the case of love, the amount of interactivity that needs to be mended is limited, allowing for natural mending. However, when one moves away from such a domain, they become exposed to a larger spectrum of interactivity, requiring a deliberate process to integrate these elements into a unified whole.

Thematic Element of Unity: Every interactive domain provides a validation of like-mindedness, establishing a natural philosophy of unity. This aids the psyche by integrating all its interactive disruptions into a unified form. The philosophical perspective of departure from love is disintegration, where reality becomes fragmented and requires reorganization in a disassembled manner. Thus, disassembly is perceived as superior to unity, and irregular interactivity follows as a result.

Contextual Regulation: An interactive domain usually has contextual regulation, even in love. When present, this context offers structural direction for interactivity, so even if deviations occur, the context persistently redirects the psyche in a single direction, preventing irregular interactivity from gaining dominance. This is similar to someone with a scheduled routine: even if deviations occur on weekends, the contextual structure of their life keeps things in balance, and over time, natural regulation takes place due to that guidance.

While we are not dismissing the importance of these aspects, we are merely explaining why they occur naturally rather than requiring manual regulation. Love, as an interactive domain, has a strict contextual direction that aligns with contemporary social understanding of its parameters. When the social context of love is removed, love descends into irregular interactivity, and even before the departure from love is complete, a departure is already fashionable due to the absence of contextual boundaries. This highlights why context is essential to an interactive domain: the loss of context results in the immediate loss of domain interactivity, which is then replaced by universal interactivity, i.e., irregular interactivity.

One might argue that manual therapeutic mending is unnecessary if one consistently remains within well-defined interactive domains, maintaining their contextual standards so that they are never faced with irregular or universal interactivity. While this is often the case, when the interactive domain is questioned or destabilized, it triggers the irregular interactivity of the universal realm. At that point, individuals become vulnerable to the instability of these systems, and as they break down, so do the individuals who depended on them. Nonetheless, it is always possible to enter a space of irregular interactivity, which brings its own challenges but also the potential for therapeutic mending. However, this mending requires conscious effort.

IV.2 A DYNAMIC SEPARATION: DOMESTICATION AND AMELIORATION

A dynamic separation consists of the amelioration of both conscious continuums and ameliorative interactivity. This entails a twofold process: first, domestication, realizing consciousness throughout the infantile layers of the psyche; and second, a deep awareness and expression of interactivity, allowing it to become ameliorative.

Unlike simplistic therapeutic repair, true amelioration must transform the narrative structure so that it emerges as wholesome. Yet, this sense of wholeness can only arise when domestication takes its natural course. Through the distribution of conscious material, the wholesome quality becomes thorough and genuine.

Two Forms of Forgiveness

.There are two forms of forgiveness: one that precedes domestication and one that emerges upon a mature prospect. The former is ineffective because its wholeness rests merely on an agreement concerning present interactivity, not on the lineage of consciousness. Consequently, it tends to repeat itself in future interactions without any substantive change. Since the foundational material is rooted in a consciousness source, interactivity will resurface as if no forgiveness had occurred. The only way to dissolve this source is through domestication; no other process yields that depth of justice, especially within interactivity.

Lineage of Consciousness and Justice

As noted in previous works, interactivity that has been ameliorated (for example, fashioned as a repository of forgiveness) reveals the lineage of consciousness and highlights its disparities. The heightened anxiety often following amelioration or forgiveness stems from this exposure; it acts as a spotlight on the consciousness lineage and the disparities it carries.

Thus, while early forms of amelioration and forgiveness can sustain one's efforts, they do not alter the consciousness source. Only domestication can achieve that transformation. Domestication enables the consciousness substance to reach its destination: the end of the psyche's layered, infantile stages. Once it arrives, it loses purpose, and its vitality diminishes. Its persistence was due only to the absence of domestication; indeed, some conscious elements would dissipate rapidly if domestication were allowed to take effect.

The Cyclical Nature of Domestication

This domestication process is far from simple; it follows distinct sequences and cycles that cannot be manipulated or redirected. Any premature attempt to restructure the process only delays the consciousness substance from reaching its natural endpoint.

For this reason, amelioration reaches true wholesomeness only when it follows domestication. After domestication has taken effect, and part of the consciousness substance has arrived at its endpoint, the next phase is the amelioration of interactivity itself; specifically, the expression of what was once living consciousness, now subdued but still reverberating within interactivity.

This interactivity marks the final trace of life within the consciousness substance; thus, amelioration becomes a farewell to its memory and presence in the psyche. However, amelioration should not merely encapsulate emotional residue; it must involve a narrative renewal. A new consciousness head must lead the interactivity, since the previous one is no longer operative. In other words, although interactivity carries the last spark of the original consciousness, it can only be completed through amelioration when a new consciousness leadership emerges. Without this transition, the result is a stagnant emotional residue, lacking lineage and drifting without purpose.

More troubling is the sentimental residue of existence itself; the lingering resentment caused by the very occurrence of consciousness substance. This existential discomfort does not vanish even after domestication, because it lacks a destination. It is not consciousness per se, but existential being; it harbors the unease of differentiation, making being itself uneasy with its own unfolding.

There is no complete domestication except through one's annihilation; where reaching the final destination means confronting the void of being. To approach wholesome amelioration, one must account for this reality. The method is narrative reshaping. Such reshaping leads to the recognition of a wholesome state of being, including the discomfort specific to consciousness. This is what we call *gratitude*. In this way, gratitude becomes both the conclusion of a wholesome and singular interactivity and the conscious-led narrative that affirms its truth.

Put simply: gratitude is the conscious effort of silent amelioration, while amelioration generates emotional interactivity. Gratitude is the conscious assent to this interactivity, guided by a narrative lens that leads the process.

IV.3 Source Material vs. Differentiation in Interactivity

Part of the therapeutic mending process is the agreement of all components that manifest as interactive material. Therefore, a thorough narrative becomes essential for that agreement, since we can attribute any experience to be the differentiation of another—or, for that matter, the source material of another.[6] It is only a matter of perspective and narrative imposition that gives an interactive element the ability to be considered source material rather than differentiation.

When an interactive element is considered differentiation, it cannot reach a conclusion with other interactive elements. This is the rule of nature: differentiation is differentiated and always remains so unless it is perceived as something else. Differentiation remains differentiated because it is only an inference from a certain dearth of source material and contains no substance of its own. Being substance-less, it cannot act as an entity to which amelioration of interactive elements is directed.

Amelioration is only possible with reference to the source material from which the differentiation gains vitality. However, doing so requires disrupting the narrative that gives the differentiation any credence. As long as differentiation is considered an existent reality; something in its own right, where its source material is only a part of

---

[6] The concept of source material and differentiation are two sides of a coin, and in metaphorical terms are 'shadow' and 'light'. It may help the reader understand that source material is the 'light' in which it does not need or propose more than itself because it is sourced in itself. As well, that differentiation is the proposal that departs from a source material, to gain a vantage point that both points to 'light' but remains in the 'shadow'.

the equation; it retains a stature that is unavailable for amelioration within the interactive experience.

Source material can be ameliorated because they originate from the same source. No argument can be made to isolate a part of the source material as a fully separate entity, deserving of thorough differentiation. Suffice it to say, with this natural law in mind, that for therapeutic mending to occur, we must surpass any narrative that differentiates interactive elements. If we proceed anyway, incorporating differentiated elements into the rest, then the final product is an amelioration without those elements, even if the experience appears wholesome.

Forgiveness and Inference

Consider a forgiveness ceremony. After a long reign of hostility, there is finally an agreement of forgiveness. Even when the experience seems complete, an underlying resentment can remain; these are the differentiation aspects. At the moment of change, they continue to remain differentiated because they are bound to a narrative that does not allow for amelioration. True forgiveness occurs only when the differentiated elements of each interactive component are acknowledged and removed from the narrative which sustains their differentiation. In doing so, all interactive elements can be rightly attributed to a specific source material. Then, the final forgiveness is truly wholesome, for there is no differentiation.

This is not to say that all resentment is a differentiation element. If there is a valid reason to remain hostile, then that hostility is a substance of source material; it represents one's own expansion being sought, and perhaps the other's as well. Amelioration, in that case, is still possible.

The differentiation elements are those that are bound into a narrative encapsulation that, instead of postulating for itself, for instance, the expansion of oneself; are the inference of a source material. For instance, because one cannot expand themselves, they become bound to a specific interactive experiences. This introduces a second mode of causality: what originates from source material becomes the determination of a differentiation, which then stands as an entity in its own right due to its causal basis. If a causal effect lies outside one's control or ability to maintain, it transforms into a differentiation; gaining the status of an independent entity by virtue of being a causal effect that does not originate from one's own state of existence.

This differs from source material elements, which are always sourced by the subjective experience of one's existence, so that the causal effect, as in the case of one's expansion having met hostility; is caused by being existent. The mere fact of existing, alongside its expansive quality, stands in opposition to that existence, presenting us with two elements of source material that remain unresolved due to the explosive nature of individuality and existence. Because the attribute of the friction is only available by a solitary subjective existence, there is no possibility to recognize that element to be an entity of its own regard. Reality is not presumed in the occasion, only the experience of existence; and how one perceives reality does not affect the outcome of the proposition of this interactive element.

Everything changes with differentiation. Since it is based solely on an inference from source material, it does not display its connection to that material for a particular reason. In the literal sense, differentiation is simply a way of describing the absence of source material, and we call it an "entity" because we are using the term "differentiation." If we had used the phrase "absence of source material," it would not be considered an entity. The moment we grant validity to an inference, rather than the material it refers to, we enter the realm of differentiation.

The only justification for this is to mark it as a reality so that it is recalled. By using the word "differentiation," we grant it a kind of autonomy and credibility. In the realm of interactive elements, differentiation rests on the justification of giving credence to its inferencing aspect. This allows us to follow a sequential narrative or maintain a focus on a specific experience of source material; one that seems deserving of more attention. However, this can only be achieved if we approach it through its differentiation, meaning we follow it based on inference. While inference is a powerful tool, enabling us to extend the qualities of material, within the realm of differentiation of interactive elements, it can be problematic.

To start, we may hold onto a portion of source material because it is presumed to be a differentiation rather than the source itself. One can view any interactive experience as differentiation instead of source material, which would then be inferencing rather than remaining true to itself. While the aspect is fundamentally source material, if it is seen as a differentiation, it becomes an act of inference.

The issue deepens when we realize that any portion of source material can be regarded as a differentiation depending on the scale and context. Hence, it's reasonable to say that any source material might be viewed as differentiation since it could be a variation of a larger body of source material. However, even when viewed as a differentiation of something insurmountable, it retains its essence as a differentiation, an entity in itself, inferred.

When conceal a justification; say, a small sum of currency as a differentiation of a larger sum, and an even larger sum for an even bigger one; there is no need to consider the inference any further. If both the small and large sums are merely inferences, we must return to the source material to settle the matter. Given the never-ending cycle of reinterpretation, we must recognize whether we are viewing the interactive element as an inference or as a portion of source material itself.

A small sum can be seen as source material for an even smaller sum, despite the prevailing belief that it is merely a differentiation. Yet, we cannot attribute all interactive elements to be source material, as the value of inference holds its own purpose. Without recognizing the small sum as the differentiation for the larger sum, one might fall into mediocrity, believing everything is flawless before a process commences.

Differentiation is necessary, as it helps understand the gradation of source material and provides a sense of direction. It is rather the occasion that one should recognize their subjective position, so that they follow the sentiment and the elements of their makeup. In each interactive element, one can assure whether the experience was really one of inference, or simply a manner of approaching source material.

The small sum can be understood subjectively, either as the experience of source material hidden to infer a larger sum, or as a disruptive experience arising from the necessity of the larger sum. In the latter case, by attributing the inference as non-consequential, and instead viewing the small sum as source material for an even smaller sum, the experience becomes consequential to one's innate perception. The experience, then, is that of inference, and we subdue this in order to fulfill an experience of source material.

Reclaiming Wholesome Subjectivity

Even when we do gain an understanding that it is in fact source material to a smaller sum, we have moved away from the subjective state and must rely on perceptual information and empathetic drives to gain that perspective. The innate experience does not function this way, and it will not be dispelled as an inference unless another mode of affairs is adopted. This requires a path of development where innate differentiation is necessary, so that in the outcome, we can truly display that it is source material; not because it is greater than a smaller sum, but because of its inherent value that transcends the inference to a larger sum. The entire narrative structure of value can shift so that it loses its inferential value and is seen as something entirely different.

However, there are times when we experience an interactive substance not through immediate inference, but rather as source material, which is then subdued for its inferential value. Sometimes, it might simply be the case that the experience is not wholesome, so the lack of source material causes the experience to become inferential, rather than representing a smaller portion of experienced source material.

This is purely based on subjective experience. It can happen that the experience was not endured as a ceremony of source material, but rather as inferential and differentiated from the very beginning. This switch can happen rapidly, causing the moment of source material to be forgotten in favor of inferring a more wholesome source material. However, because the initial moment is as it is, it remains fundamentally a source material construction.

In most cases, there will be elements of both source material and differentiation; some that infer toward broader source material and others that are experienced as source material in themselves. Yet, we are often predisposed to follow the differentiation, as it is there that we can progress in our autonomous selves. Because of this, we adopt a narrative of the whole experience. The experience usually takes on a unified form, so if it is inferred, then that is the case; but if it is the source material itself, then that becomes the outlook.

If we were to presume an experience containing inferential material to be the source material, we would lose the prerogative of following the genuine nature of our subjective experiences. If this matter continues unchecked, the entire perception of what constitutes a good or proper experience would be corrupted, and the subjective self would no longer participate in the view. Without such differentiation, we lose our complexity and self-awareness, becoming unable to discern different intellectual materials, thus not knowing what to attend to.

Alternatively, if we assume the wholesome experience to be inferential material without recognizing and accepting its source material, we build a resentment portfolio owing to the complex differentiation and constant self-critique, always seeking beyond current stature. If everything is merely inference, the entire makeup of one's current value becomes an enlarged differentiation. This will lead to resentment in interactive experiences, as the inference lacks vitality of its own and is ultimately dependent on the source material; a source material that is seen as unattainable due to one's current stature, despite being the very force that energizes the entire affair.

Differentiation as Intellectual Danger

This is why we often find those more intellectually inclined to be more hostile in disposition: it is their constant engagement with the differentiation of intellectual material, which is simply an inference to source material. Being on the side of inference causes one to embody the differentiation of the concerned subject, so that we are engaging in the differentiation of *therapeutic mending*. We differentiate because we can engage with it more deeply, but in doing so, we are simply inferring what wholesome is from the vantage point of non-wholesomeness.

The conclusion of this subject would not be more differentiation from the subject, but rather a departure from the material in order to return to a wholesome state; while considering the details that were learned. Even as we sit on the sidelines to differentiate within the subject, we gain vitality only because of our experiences as being wholesome. We might venture to state that someone who does not have an inclination toward a wholesome nature would not be able to partake in this intellectual exercise. Even the term "intellectual exercise" highlights that the outcome of such exercise is for the sake of health or growth, an outcome where a wholesome experience is the ultimate goal.

The question then becomes: When is differentiation appropriate, and when is source material appropriate? First, we have noted that subjective experience is paramount. For one individual, the initial interactive experience may have been differentiation, while for another, it could have been source material. The genuine outplay of the experience depends on how it is approached.

We can determine that the source material is the true experience only when it is the experience which was initially encountered. Because of the subconscious layers and their complexity, any experience involves a negotiation as to whether it is source material or inferential; and an argument can be made for either. However, we do not concern ourselves with justifying this, but rather with how it manifests in real time. If one follows the inferential material with such variety, building worldviews around it until it eventually becomes source material, then that will be the manifest interactive material. Until then, the experience will be aligned with the initial experience.

Therefore, the initial experience is constantly evolving based on its inferential value. For instance, a small sum might have been experienced as inferential to a larger sum, but if an economic collapse occurs and larger sums lose their relevance, the original experience, as it was initially understood; would no longer be constitute a revisit. The worldview that offered meaning to that inference is gone, so the inferential value is lost, and it is no longer an inference.

IV.4 EMPATHY, CODEPENDENCY, AND THE ILLUSION OF UNITY

We are inclined to view the mending process as inclusive of all social elements, particularly the measures of validation in the psyche. These social elements are specific to whatever manifests from the exposed aspects of the psyche but also include any external perceptions that are influenced by the interactive domain. At any given moment, the individual ruminates and activates interactive material based on the sociality of their historical precedent.

The perceptual domain also interacts with a social system, which is a validating measure that reflects the individual's interactive system. Whatever the exposed elements of the individual psyche, the perceptual domain will reflect upon them to provide a social validation of that basis. When there is interactive irregularity in the individual psyche, the accordance and affordance of the perceptual domain will validate that irregularity, so it is as if one is interacting with the external realm as if it were a social being. Hence, whenever we discuss therapeutic mending, we must recognize two social actualities: one representing the multiple social elements of the psyche pertaining to the individual, and the other, the external realm as a social actuality validating those very elements.

When one includes another social being in the therapeutic mending process, it leads to the assumption that all the interactive material, highly personal to the individual psyche, partakes in that external social entity as if it were an internal aspect of the system.

Already, we are perplexed by the assumption that any therapeutic mending process of particular psyche fragments would create a system in which each part assumes the internality of the other. In other words, even within the psyche itself, when the therapeutic mending process culminates, these interactive psychic fragments of varying degrees are now treating all their voices as internal, despite their origins in various historical precedents.

Emotional Mending and Social Perception

The therapeutic process can manifest naturally, as experienced through crying, mourning, pity, empathy, sympathy, and other mending emotional states. For our purposes, they perform similarly. So, when one cries, they are mending a distinct part of their interactive process related to shock. This may occur at the infantile stage to reconcile with an uncooperative reality, but doing so in the form of an aggrieved disheartening of that very mending. This is why crying can last for a prolonged period; it can be the antithesis of the very thing it seeks to accomplish. In other words, it is trying to mend, but resists doing so, which leads to an ensemble of tears.

Mourning follows the same pattern, except that the portions involved are more sophisticated. One side represents attachment, and the other, inevitable detachment. These forces seek resolution, yet each part desires to remain as it is. Pity, whether directed at oneself or others, is the resolution of a state of interactivity that is challenging to believe; meaning a part is disbelieved, even though there is substantial evidence of its realness. Mending in this case is a state of pity, which can endure for a prolonged period if disbelief or unwillingness to accept reality recurrently resists the evidence that places that reality in question. Empathy and sympathy both involve mending the wholeness of other social beings, or at least a deep attachment of certain aspects of social beings. This process involves mending others to become a singularity by way of them, or at least with certain aspects of them.

At once, we notice a fair distinction between the process where one becomes a singularity with another due to an aspect or role they embody, rather than egregiously attending to the totality of their personhood. For instance, a family member in conflict with another may reach a place of empathy to resolve the issue at hand. In the proper sense, empathy reflects an awareness of the depth of reality intended for a universal agreement to the experience of that issue. The empathetic individual is merely a bridge for the other person to understand the state of mind and subjective experience of the issue, attaching to the part of themselves that does not fully understand the depth of the contender's position.

When this process turns into what we mistakenly call "mending," it transpires when the wholeness of a person's identity, the entire "poor" person; becomes the point of attachment. Instead of merely imagining what it would be like to be poor, it becomes about imagining what it would be like to be this specific individual who concurrently is poor.

The Trap of Full-Self Fusion

This is the call to action for an entire mending of selfhood, which immediately results to codependency. The individual then becomes an internality within the other person's identity, thereby participating in the appearance of perpetuating the internal emotional sphere.

This occurs because, even if one agrees that the initial investigation was based on the "poor" aspect, it creates a sense that they are only using the other person for the embodied experience of that aspect. Rather than learning about the embodiment of poverty, one feels compelled to internalize the entire landscape of that individual's experience. It's often the case that poverty is accompanied by problematic moral systems, and so, in the role of empathizer, one inadvertently participates in these moral systems, ironically replacing the very moral framework that promotes sympathy.

The mending process is meant to create a fusion between two distinct parts; parts that are already present, that are not going away, and that require resolution for the stability of continuity within the individual. However, it is not necessarily the interactive parts that requisite mending; rather, it is a deeper understanding and resolution between two points of consciousness.

For instance, if someone has endured a particular consciousness formed by their infantile experience of development, and then, within the realm of maturity, acquires another consciousness, one typically separate and distinct from the infantile stage; the result is a conflict. This conflict can be resolved through the mending process, with empathy towards the infantile stage or through any other mechanism that facilitates an emotional process, allowing those two interactive elements to merge into a singularity. However, there still remains the element of consciousness from both realms. An entire intellectual database was established during the infantile stage, all which does not simply recede due to emotional fusion.

Consider the case of royal siblings, one crowned as king and the other made archduke. Despite emotional intimacy and a bond of likeness, there is still a distinction: one is the royal leader, and the other is secondary. These are two distinct consciousness manifestations that can only be fundamentally resolved through the departure of one. There could be a process in which the archduke comes to understand the experience of being crowned, and the king; the experience of being the archduke. This understanding can lead to a resolution, but deprived of complete enmeshment, because the distinction between these two roles is vast.

This is why we can never reach a true resolution unless the crowned individual agrees that both roles are distinctly competent in their positions. However, this can only happen if the archduke arrives at this conclusion through intellectual understanding. Therefore, any bonding that occurs will only serve to highlight the separation between these distinctions, creating more interactive elements that will require further bonding.

This is the reality of therapeutic mending, if followed too thoroughly, it only amplifies the distinctiveness of each consciousness source, which leads to even more emotive experiences. The hope is that, with such a process in place, the highlighted elements can reach a deeper degree of resolution between the dynamic spaces of the two points of consciousness. However, it is usually the case that the distinctiveness of consciousness is vast, making it unlikely to reach intellectual conclusions or empathetic understanding for each side.

In the case of the infantile and mature stages, they can reach an empathetic understanding, nevertheless this understanding tends to fade over time, despite all the intellectual data supporting it. This is because the understanding of that dynamic space is inevitably distinct, and after a period of understanding, each side naturally leans toward its fundamental nature. This is one reason why family-building is required after the departure from the infantile stage; it provides a reservoir of data that clarifies one's infantile stage as a dynamic process. If there were a simple solution, it would have been found by now. However, because distinct conscious elements can never reach a full resolution, this process becomes necessary.

The question, then, becomes: what creates further separation between two consciousness sources, and what makes this separation less significant? To answer this, we turn to the archduke analogy. The disparity is great because each role plays a significant part in the social system. As each point of consciousness becomes enlarged through its role, the opposing point is experienced with greater disparity. A mature individual who relies on their maturity for a significant role in the social system will experience a greater disparity between their stages of maturity and infancy. The disparity grows in proportion to the demand of the social system for that position of maturity. A regular individual might not perceive this disparity as pronounced, but once placed in a high position within the social system, the distance between maturity and infancy is significantly enlarged.

We arrive at another conclusion: the position of points of consciousness varies depending on one's awareness of themselves within the context of a social system. We could even say that the more pertinent an individual is to the social system, the greater the disparity between their consciousness parts. However, it is not the social system itself that creates this self-awareness; rather, it is the individual's ability to enlarge their sense of self. This self-awareness is heightened due to the quid pro quo nature of the social system. The social system does not enlarge the disparity between the king and the archduke; instead, it is the self-adapted awareness of the individual system that notices the great distance between personal parts and interpersonal dynamic spheres. Any individual can adapt their self-awareness, enlarging their sense of individuality according to their perception, which in turn creates this same disparity.

Therefore, an individual may have intellectually understood the dynamic between the infantile and mature stages, but due to a lack of self-adapted awareness, they may not fully grasp the depth of the disparity between the two. Upon gaining new awareness, they may then recognize the greater disparity, realizing that their previous understanding was insufficient to bridge the gap between the two stages.

What is really happening is that the awareness and self-understanding of the mature stage has developed immensely, which makes the inflection point of infancy seem distant. The prior understanding no longer suffices to provide a dynamic exchange. This is why the role of the "homebody" becomes even more important as this self-adapted process expands, whether through the individual or the social system.

IV.5 RITUALIZATION AND THE CULTURAL NEED FOR MENDING

Because therapeutic mending is an important process of the progressive era of civilization, it becomes the breeding ground for its formalization in a ritualistic manner; ensuring it is neither forgotten nor neglected. We can feel a certain sympathy toward this historical choice, as one is prone to neglect participating in something that enters the domain of the psyche and molds aspects together; especially as there is no logical formulation that supports this process, and it often runs counter to logical presuppositions.

Why Ritual Emerges from Psychological Need

The psyche is not formulated to mend its interactivity, nor is the rational notion to provide any assistance, for each interactive notion is deserving of its own credence, rather than being seen as an ensemble of varying pieces that should be included in a single encapsulation. Instead, only a theory of reality that centers the consciousness continuum will be able to teach the psyche that the process of mending is paramount; so that one may arrive at an encapsulation that aligns with themselves as a singularity. Without that singularity of interactivity, there is no present state to the individual, nor proper choices in regard to the attention given to specific interactive components.

Singular Identity and Structured Selfhood

The psyche does not inherently know how to manage interactive irregularities or how to distribute material and attention according to a systematic framework. Such provision would require a system; a method to stipulate the level of attention each part receives and, more importantly, a conclusive placement of selfhood as a settled singularity. This can only occur when there is a procedure in place to mend and ameliorate interactive elements, granting them a unified structure through which one's identity and functional coherence can emerge.

In the absence of this, one relies on the assumption that the natural voice of each interactive aspect, upon its inclusion into a shared space, will form a kind of kinship with a specific allotment. That allotment is aligned with bedrock reality, where the nature of its portion is afforded based on its realist stature as a substance.

This is comparable to a relationship, where the state prior consisted of two distinct entities, and where an amelioration occurs that allows the individuals to become voiced as a single entity. This singular voice of the relationship includes both entities, but the allotment is afforded not on equal terms, but in accordance with the consciousness continuum of genuine reality. This is not a choice on behalf of the parties, since they have already become an encapsulation; rather, it is the formulation of reality itself and its nuanced recognitions that give proper proportions their due credit. There is no other entity that can direct that singularity, and the two parties no longer have distinct voices; external entities remain external, never given recognition to be more than that.

Performance vs. Reality in Social Bonds

There are instances, however, where one party may take the responsibility of direction in that amelioration, thereby disregarding the mending process itself. They may appear as if they are part of a singularity, when in fact they are a distinct entity seeking to regulate the relationship. In such cases, this is merely a process of manipulation, where two distinct entities endure an experience that is separated and not mended; one taking direction with their façade, and the other following with theirs. Both are in agreement to the recreation of singularity only when they proceed as distinct individuals.

The same applies to therapeutic mending. Individuals may believe they have resolved their interactive irregularities and advocate themselves as a singularity. In this event, they may present themselves as a formulated system, when in fact there is irregular interactivity broiling under the surface. The ability to maintain the appearance of amelioration is then achieved by contextually oppressing interactive exposure. This contextual procedure may not stem from any real inclination toward the context, but rather be used as a mechanism of mending, or more accurately, repression, allowing them to function without the disturbance of irregular interactivity.

We may notice a tendency where the chosen domain of context is one that offers little personal alignment. In this way, it does not threaten interactivity because of its distance from personhood. However, in such cases, there is little development for the psyche from this context, due to its lack of evocative connection; its only utility being to circumvent the broiling interactivity threatening exposure. Upon fatigue, weakness, or other limitations, when one cannot maintain a contextual direction; they fall into a ditch of irregular interactivity. Only upon regaining strength can they reassert their interactive claim and endure unabated.

The same is true for relationships that use context to perform as an amelioration, when in reality the parties are merely distinct entities performing as if they are mended. For example: friendships maintained for accessibility, or marriages sustained for social gain. The ability to maintain and retain the relationship comes from non-relational material. There exists a fair-bonding context that holds them together and sustains equilibrium, but this context is the only maintenance of that relationship.

The use of contexts to appear as though one is mending may suffice temporarily. It is not always the case that someone is available to unaffectedly mend their interactivity, nor are couples always ready to endure a true relationship amelioration. What is required instead is a context that maintains exposure and keeps erratic interactivity at bay. In its proper form, it becomes a useful tool; allowing one to continue a day, a week, or a month under the premise of amelioration, despite the simmering irregularity beneath.

We often find that couples who maintain no contextual systems, and who rely entirely on amelioration and relational foundations; find themselves fatigued. It is not always possible to be available for continuous system-mending or for sustaining singularity, especially not over prolonged periods. Instead, they must rely on a contextual bridge that presumes singularity, when in truth irregular interactivity makes them distinct and separate.

The same is true for individuals. The psyche is not always able to mend all its irregular formulations and instead relies on contextual systems to keep interactivity at bay, allowing functional continuity through their "contexts of mending." However, the usual case is that these are not used as tools, but instead are relied on in extremes: either to present an illusion of continuous mending with no definite availability for proper resolution, or with complete disregard; construing the contextual system ineffective as a haven for the ongoing exposures.

IV.6 The Limits and Risks of Therapeutic Unification

This leads us to the other side, that of a class of individuals who participate in conscious rumination but are not part of distinct interactive domains. For them, it would be the case that they are exposed to consciousness regularly, so that interactivity is highly developed. However, this does not transform into irregular interactivity because the individual may attach to present consciousness without suitable separation. As a result, it would represent the topmost of the consciousness continuum that does not nurture interactive inferences unrelated to the current existential landscape. Although interactivity is highly exposed, it aligns with the continuous present moment of consciousness, where all inferences are put on hold to passage the sequence forward.

In this way, the entire attachment to the continuum becomes a safe haven for irregular interactivity. It would not expose anything unrelated to present consciousness and its cogitation. The only manner in which consciousness exposes all interactivity is when it is in a process of interaction with consciousness itself, entering and departing, so that each reentry reveals the entire existential landscape of the individual, rather than merely having their individuality become a part of the continuation of consciousness.

This is why it is fairly common to find that those who impart to the continuum do so with their entire individuality. They do not make exceptions, especially with familial members, because they expose their individuality, which does not align with the continuum.

Additionally, the disruption of the continuum seems problematic. Why would one depart from the reservoir of reality and its measure to enter into individuality, especially if this will only expose their interactivity along the landscape of their entire existential selves, subject to validation for prominence and control, all at the mercy of the individual and their equilibrium?

Overexposure and Disintegration

This is where therapeutic mending arrives. It is this process that can provide the much-needed support, allowing one to depart and reenter consciousness at will, all without perturbing irregular interactivity. Irregular interactivity will become an element, but therapeutic mending will mold those exposed elements in a way that creates a singular and present interactive encapsulation for the continuation of interaction with consciousness.

When interactivity within the experience of consciousness becomes irregular, therapeutic mending must occur without resorting to conscious rumination. In fact, such rumination is counterproductive, as persistent cogitation only further illuminates the interactive domain, thereby intensifying the conscious dimension rather than soothing it. Since interactivity, particularly when governed by the immediacy of the present; is largely propelled by consciousness itself, attempts at mending will not resolve the irregularities within the interactive structure of experience. Instead, they amplify the very interaction they aim to correct, exposing it to greater consciousness and, in turn, deepening the irregularity.

This is why we must consider the principle of departing from conscious rumination, or, alternatively, the effect of recreating a container for consciousness; as a means of offering refuge for therapeutic mending. When mending takes place within the field of consciousness, it is consciousness itself that becomes exposed to the psyche, rather than the underlying need for mending that precedes conscious awareness. Worse, the momentum gained through mending or exposure to more consciousness will absorb the irregular interactivity into that encapsulation, thereby making consciousness responsible for receiving the irregular interactivity and its measures of consciousness. This disrupts the process of conscious integration and includes irregular aspects, resulting in a non-sequential consciousness that derives from prior elements of the system.

The mending of an interactive exposure can be done through unification via empathy, which is inclusive of those pockets of interaction. It can also be done incorrectly, where a specific interactive point becomes the center upon which all other points are attempted to be mended. Instead of including all of them in equal, non-particular measure, mending can focus on one point that requires more attention. We see this when an individual engages in conversation or social interaction, allowing for validation and recognition of that particular point. Although there may be a manifestation of mending across the interactive spectrum of the psyche, focusing on this point can cause an injustice, as it would neglect other aspects of the psyche and reveal more interactivity within that single point.

This could lead to a perpetual process in which one continues to validate that point, only to be exposed to more interactivity. There would be no end to this particular interactive point, as it would expand to microscopic proportions and repeatedly gain more significance. By disproportionately focusing on this point, it would direct the persona in forward motion. Because the vitality of an interactive voice relies on the information that has been overexposed to the psyche, individuals would continuously seek validation in sustaining that voice.

In the usual case, where there is no specific focus on a point, the finality of the interactive voice does not need constant maintenance. There is natural justice throughout the psyche for the various interactive pockets, and once the mending has been achieved, there is no need to revisit those pockets for revalidation. However, this process of unification is for the sake of interactive homogeneity, not for the objective truth of the system. Interactive pockets are to remain separated until enough conceptual connections are made to allow their unity to be foolproof.

The reality of the psyche is not unified. Even as there are elements and meta-elements that align, a remaining separation persists. We can say that an interactive pocket is no longer such when the consciousness that produced its contents and present sequential consciousness are aligned. If we were to revisit the state of mind of that interactive pocket, it would agree wholeheartedly with that revision, dismissing its prior proposition to be included into the current system. This can only occur through dynamic exchanges, conceptual arrangements, and other methods.

The Infantilization of Complex Pockets

There are some interactive pockets that can never be unified, so it may not be the resolution to seek complete mending. These pockets contain so much nuance and separation that they must remain as they are. We are discussing therapeutic mending in the context of momentary exposure of interactive elements that require mending, allowing the interactive base to emerge.

This is why we find certain forms of social amity to be troubling. Not because therapeutic mending is not a wholesome endeavor, but when it is treated as a means of unifying reality, it can lead to a degenerative spiral. The constant amelioration of interactive substance eventually declines conceptual complexity and consciousness itself.

With such veracity to the amelioration, all interactive exposure will not be allowed nuanced development but will immediately be thrust into amelioration. Those interactive pockets will eventually lose the notion of them constituting pockets at all owing to the compulsive unification, and so will the consciousness which had produced them. When an interactive pocket is stripped away as a distinctive element of the psyche, it loses its sincerity and dynamic elements, so that it cannot provide that voice for the interactive landscape.

As we have noted, when there is therapeutic mending, we gain an interactive voice that includes all these various aspects, but its vitality is reliant upon the interactive pockets and their distinctiveness, which offers justification for its proportion to that wholesome voice. When we compulsively unify, the pocket itself as a source, loses its ability of distinctiveness; thus loses its stability, so that the interactive voice cannot include its informational elements.

The forward-looking voice of interactivity becomes less intricate as more pockets become submerged and unavailable to participate. Since interactive pockets contain the consciousness of one's development, the submerged consciousness will also lose its productivity. The result is a simplified interactive landscape and a consciousness encapsulation that is adrift, dependent solely on the present surroundings for any vitality.

If that is not enough of a letdown, a manifestation of resentment will arise from this compulsive drive toward unification. This resentment emerges from certain interactive pockets that resist unification; not out of defiance, but due to their inherent complexity or formative structure. Typically, these are infantile pockets of interaction that, despite all efforts, remain unmeasurable because of existential gaps, for example, those found in child-parent or sibling-sibling relationships. These gaps are natural and resist integration.

Such pockets may surface, but rather than contributing to a sophisticated continuum, they stand exposed; raw and unmediated, like an infant speaking. This kind of exposure, which cannot be resolved or reabsorbed into the larger structure, becomes the dominant force in interactivity. Lacking the full complexity of consciousness, individuals are unable to discern or meaningfully direct these interactions. The result is a growing resentment, rooted precisely in these points of failed development.

Such individuals do not become a troubling social phenomenon because they lack the complexity to envision anything beyond their resentment. However, they become vulnerable to external influence from social figures who lack discernment, allowing this resentment to manifest in problematic social contexts. This often emerges in certain gatherings, where individuals express their underlying resentment, disguised as unity; through compulsive acts of mending. In such cases, the true atmosphere is one of resentment rather than unity.

If they are engaged in a way that begins to foster a collective sentiment, the foundational tone of the entire group becomes rooted in resentment. In doing so, the group participates in a form of consciousness shaped by that resentment. Such groupings often exist apart from civilized structures, as they seek consciousness without engaging in the self-reflection or rumination that typically accompanies it. This pursuit often leads them to desert-like locales, both literal and metaphorical; where they can entertain a form of consciousness that feels unique to them but is, in fact, infused with infantile resentment. This resentment then reflects back upon them in increasingly distorted ways.

Any social cause grounded in great unity or amelioration becomes a breeding ground for such resentment, replacing the unity it ostensibly seeks. It's as if individuals bring their unresolved negativity into a space designed for restorative growth, only to actualize that negativity more fully.

Authentic Mending vs. Performative Healing

The key distinction here is that therapeutic mending is not aimed at unifying the psyche or relationships in a lasting way, but rather at engaging with the interactivity of the present moment. True therapeutic mending cannot occur if it is tied to objectives of actualization or the pursuit of heightened consciousness, as understood by those who seek solitude in desert-like spaces. In such cases, cogitation becomes part of the mending process itself, so that instead of gaining clarity or cohesion, one ends up with a heightened state of consciousness that merely amplifies scattered points of interaction as the psyche's direction.

In some cases, gatherings in such isolated locales may aim for amelioration without the burden of regular cognitive succession. Yet, because any gathering inevitably produces a shared field of consciousness, a dilemma arises. The only way social amelioration can occur outside of collective consciousness is through the individual; by focusing not on performative unity but on the exposure and integration of the psyche's interactive elements.

The same principle applies to any attempt at collective unity. If the gathering seeks to unify on a social level, it falls into the same pitfalls described above. But if its purpose is to unify the interactive dimensions of individual psyches, it can serve as a model for what proper social interaction might look like.

However, when therapeutic mending is taken too far, the individual pockets of interactivity, and their underlying material; are pressured to reveal even more. This does not mean any single interactive thread becomes dominant; rather, the entire landscape of exposed content becomes stretched thin in an effort to create a more coherent whole. This process can backfire: overexposure leads to irregular interactivity during subsequent episodes of engagement, resulting in a kind of breakdown due to excessive, un-contextualized expression.

If the conceptual process were purposeful and structured, it would naturally guide these interactive revelations. But when too much is exposed without a conceptual framework to contain it, the excess becomes disjointed. Later efforts at amelioration then risk fracturing aspects of consciousness instead of integrating them.

SECTION V: CASE STUDY & APPLIED REFLECTIONS

V.1 MEDIA AND CONSCIOUSNESS RECREATION

Having mapped out the underlying mechanics of how consciousness can be activated and sustained through structural memory and ritual, we now turn to the realm where these mechanisms play out most visibly: media. In the following essay, we will trace how these mediated ceremonies transform passive consumption into communal participation; and how, in doing so, they both revive and domesticate consciousness.

A primary example is visual media, particularly live events, where simply being present and participating in the experience makes one a member of the event. Through subtle nuances, one serves and embodies an experience that recreates the events within the local arena. The value is ritualistic because, by attending live events, the conceptual aspect of participation makes one a participant, even while in a sedentary position. The embodiment created by live media or any "live" subsidiary provides the potential to recreate consciousness based on one's memory traces.

This is not to downplay the possibility of any media in a context that does not aim to recreate consciousness but simply memorializes its consciousness lineage. The experience becomes effective only when it carries a ritualistic element. The furthermost ritualistic media is live, due to its scheduled nature and real-time participation. Other forms of media, such as trending issues, may seem "alive" due to the social interactions surrounding them. The same can be said for news: simply engaging with a set of agreed-upon social interactions makes it ritualistic, thus embodying one's conscious memory traces. However, this is not always the case. One can avoid the ritualistic aspects, participating in media consumption merely to follow developments or for entertainment, with the awareness that the social sphere is in agreement.

We can better understand the extent of the ritualistic sense, or more accurately, the physical embodiment; by observing an individual's availability to participate. For example, in live media, the individual is participating because of the time constraints of the live creation. This inherently makes it an embodiment. Any consumption of developing media, or media expended in a way that leads to an embodied state for the individual, will inevitably result in the recreation of the memory trace, rather than merely contextual inquiry.

Media consumption itself is the amelioration of content that has reached social consciousness, creating a real-time, ritualistic sentiment to the endeavor; much like news, which is often the most pertinent setting for the embodiment of consciousness traces. Yet, to avoid these elements, i.e., to ignore their input; would not benefit the contextual systems that follow a sequential pattern of those memory traces. While memory alone can serve as a consciousness measure, it has no ramifying relevance to one's systematic function. Only through a contextual through line, sometimes a narrative; can this consciousness be brought to the forefront. Not necessarily to become an embodiment and thus a recreation, but to provide a purposeful objective to the substance. It does require a medium of movement, so if it is not settled structurally, it must endure through a contextual and sequential pattern.

For this reason, all developing media is worthwhile, as it provides direction and re-approach to one's contextual system. If the news takes a certain direction, it would benefit the individual to include such in the contextual direction. The objective of the contextual throughline is to make consciousness a more wholesome endeavor, and consciousness is dependent on the hierarchy of the structural system and, more so, on the sociality of the current moment.

One may enter the consciousness continuum that far outpaces or retreats from the sentiment of that sociality, and thus the consciousness will not endure at its fundamental reality. When arriving at the structural haven of consciousness, with their contextual system, which differs dramatically from the conceptual happenstance of the environment, one will be coerced toward the choice of higher-grade consciousness, and all that context will be lost for that aim.

There is no choice in the matter because the rule of reality is that higher-grade consciousness, when considering conceptual and structural consciousness, will outpace and override any individual or sequestered group of consciousness. Whether it outpaces or retracts, whether it reminds or fulfills a utopian ideal, it will all be lost.

When engaging in localized media or news, especially toward current sociality, it can either offer the pace of provisions for one's contextual footprint or become the embodiment of that environment, much like live events, which tend to only be embodiments. As we noted, the embodiment provides the recreation of consciousness, supplied by memory traces of consciousness inputted into the embodied consumption, so that one is not attending the live event or current sociality but merely using that as a basis for their further consciousness traces to be renewed and recreated in the current environment.

While recreation seems like the most likely use of these forms of content, instead of requiring them to be localized, domesticated, and separated from the public sphere, these forms provide the accurate and available embodiment to consciousness, and thus the recreation of consciousness. Domestication becomes a full-fledged reality that does not require any externality. However, this recreation through embodiment is the cause of future dysfunction.

First, it diminishes the possibility of entertaining the public realm outside of this domestication, for the domestication already offers that substance. Second, the recreation effect devalues and diminishes the memory trace of consciousness, bolstering the recreated element. Thus, participation in the localized realm of embodiment means the memory traces it relies upon, since it is merely dependent on them; become secondary and unnoticed, while the recreation of the experience of that locality through the consciousness conduit becomes the fortified reality.

It is a matter of approach and the level of ritualized elements within the consumption process. If the consumption does not lead to embodiment but only provides nuances to one's context; making it not entertainment in the sense of recreation, but in the sense of social alignment; then it cannot be considered recreation, nor does it have its typically negative effects. Two primary forms of consumption that already carry high levels of ritualization, live events and news consumption; require a deeper contextual engagement. This shift towards ritualization actualizes the live event within one's localized realm. Why else would one engage in live events or real-time news if not to recreate the localized realm as a conscious experience?

This process mirrors the ritualized realms within religious or other frameworks, which follow a similar structure, though with a different form of consumption. While media and social consumption can sometimes lead to embodiment and the recreation of consciousness through memory traces, the ritualized element does the same, but in a more direct embodiment state. Socialized media consumption, however, is not inherently an embodiment state. It requires both liveliness and real-time aspects, as well as a ritualized embodiment; whether in the form of a gathering, setting, or scheduling the experience.

The ritual aspect, however, is mainly structured to create a physical environment that reproduces consciousness through memory traces. While it affects embodiment as a natural process, it does not directly relate to one's conscious memory traces. Socialized media consumption is adjacent to one's universal conscious memory traces; it emanates from the same realm and participates in a dynamic, concurrent way. On the other hand, the ritualized realm follows a system that struggles to pull in these essential conscious memory traces.

It is only through complex mental effort that one can fully engage in these traditional ritualized environments and connect with their memory traces, which come from the universal realm. Fortunately, those who participate deeply in ritualized systems often do not consciously recognize their universal conscious memory traces. As a result, they cannot fully grasp the expanded consciousness they experience within the ritualized environment. If they were to engage in ritualized behavior while aware of its universal conscious memory traces, they would become a significantly vulnerable prospect. In this case, they would engage in ritualized behaviors designed to embody consciousness while also holding a complete memory of that consciousness. This leads to a localized embodiment and recreation of consciousness in a highly concurrent and probable manner.

However, even if they achieve some form of embodiment, it is not a recreation of a high level of consciousness, nor does it pertain to the individual's broader horizons. It tends to relate to more supplementary, cyclical aspects of consciousness; typically acquired during infancy. This is the system's safeguard: even if an embodiment occurs, it does not threaten the recreation of anything substantial, nor does it disrupt real consciousness that is informed by the retrieved memory traces.

On the other hand, socialized media consumption is closer to one's universal and expanding conscious memory traces. Therefore, if ritualized, it could potentially recreate and validate certain aspects of consciousness. This is why socialized media consumption does not naturally arrive with ritual; instead, it is typically a conceptual endeavor. However, some of its elements become ritualized, raising the possibility of recreating consciousness. Even in its most embodied form, whether live or in the presence of certain elements; socialized media cannot surpass the expanded consciousness, nor isolate the localized realm from its attachments to the public space.

How can we differentiate between recreation and mere contextual output based on one's choice to align with sociality for context? It comes down to the motive behind the content's use: is it to provide a sense of social reality, or to create a social reality for oneself? The same news consumption can serve as a simple update on the socialized realm or as a way to forge a semblance of vitality and consciousness to one's localized experience. We quickly notice that any form of news consumption involves an element of consciousness because it relies on one's broad memory traces to create the momentary experience of vitality and real-time awareness. It is as if one is depleted of consciousness and turns to consumption to embody that consciousness, even though they still rely on memory traces for that effect.

This, however, is not the true nature of the experience. A true embodiment of consciousness does not engage entirely with memory traces of consciousness, but rather grosses its perceptual effect in real-time, based on the environment. While most engagements with broad consciousness are informed by prior states, the extent of this is limited in comparison to earlier frameworks. However, if this experience represents the most expansive consciousness one has achieved, it will not rely on memory traces, because there are none.

The key distinction lies not in the use of memory traces but in how they are utilized. Even someone aligned with the socialized realm retains a memory trace of consciousness that is activated through participation. The difference lies in their reasoning: they are not simply browsing to enter an embodied state; they are engaging with a purposeful understanding of the socialized realm, despite the potential for embodiment that might accompany it.

V.2 CASE ANALYSIS: THE ISOLATED INDIVIDUAL AND THE VENERATION OF SOCIAL EXUBERANCE AS A CONSCIOUS GATEWAY

Introduction

In the framework of domesticated consciousness, there is a possible interplay between social isolation or perceived inferiority, and the veneration of an externally vibrant persona. This dynamic creates a space for both transference and potential pathology.

Melanie Klein (1932) addresses transference as the interpretation of the child's unconscious desires. When these desires are uncovered, the child becomes aware of their internal process through identification with the person who facilitated that awareness. This transference relates to the process of domestication, where the child becomes available for the removal of its fortified boundaries. In this case, the superego is activated as the ideal whom perceives beyond that domestication, or simple play. The superego integrates both the interpretation as a knowledge-base and as the celebrated conscious material, all tied to a social framework centered on the clinician.[7]

If the child's domestication progressed into a more sophisticated arena, perhaps with more depth and embodiment; it would involve a different process: a conscious observer who does not change the prior domestication but creates a new ideal called the superego. In this case,

---

[7] Klein, Melanie. 1932. The Psycho-Analysis of Children. London: Hogarth Press and the Institute of Psycho-Analysis.

even after interpretation, the child remains as they were in accordance with their unconscious desires but now as an onlooker, both corporeal (the perspective of the doctor) and psychological (the superego). The child now contends with the new awareness whereas their unconscious desires remain unchanged.

In essence, the child has now domesticated the persona of interpretation, not the interpretation material, because understanding is not what they are seeking but an adulted version, in which they do not need to adhere to the simple process of their neurotic state. This newfound superego did not make a fundamental change to the psyche, but does the job of becoming stern upon unconscious desires and their outlets performed in play.

Transference is inevitable because whenever they question a process, they do not enter into dialogue with that newfound interpretation, but owed to the slight realization of its contents they now perceive the doctor as the mode apparatus for their psyche. They enter into a psychological union and use them as a direction in all their complexes. So that now they are a child who has neglected their unconscious process, and follows a regiment of that persona as if it were them.

Besides the noticeable problem, a subtle difficulty arises: the individual does not receive an accurate portrayal of the clinician, but only what their agile mind can handle. This results in a general overview devoid of subtlety. Through constant questioning, what would they do? they begin a complex journey to become aware of the intricacies of the clinician.

The therapeutic anticipation is that they allow the superego to interact with their unconscious development, so that the persona of the doctor mediates the unconscious reception of material at its appropriate time. However, we must consider that transference, as a process, involves the domestication of consciousness. In cases of neurotic instability, the clinician becomes a venerated figure, upon whom all hope rests. This domesticated relationship strengthens the superego, which tallies the individual, yet it is simply the reception of social constructs against the desires and processes of the natural psyche. In extreme cases, this may cause the individual to expel their psychological process entirely, leaving only the dialogue of the superego.

This case analysis explores an individual who, feeling socially sequestered or inferior, turns to an exuberant, socially adept figure as a "conscious gateway." While we typically view consciousness as a rumination or structural element, in cases of confinement, the individual might perceive this figure as a doorway to the realm of consciousness. This is a common situation of domesticated consciousness, where we regard the individual's experience of confinement to understand the veneration placed upon the admired figure.

For instance, a dignitary may be venerated, but it is uncommon for someone to domesticate their persona unless their environment is so lacking that the figure becomes the sole outlet for consciousness. In this case it could be anyone, chosen simply because they are the most accessible and well-known.

The sequestered individual embarks on a process of domestication, selectively internalizing the admired persona's core attributes; general aspects that shape their own development. By doing so, they shift their focus from an intrinsic sense of self toward defining their identity solely in relation to the other.

A critical element that interrupts this process is the social buffer, a psychic mechanism that acknowledges two key realities:

Partiality of Consciousness: Every individual represents only a fragment of consciousness. No single person can encapsulate the totality of another's experiential and developmental fabric. The "gateway" figure should be seen merely as an entranceway, not a destination.

Preservation of the Self: The buffer preserves one's dynamic flow, preventing complete identification with the other. It ensures that integration occurs selectively rather than through total absorption.

In contrast, codependency is characterized by enmeshment, where personal boundaries dissolve. This is not an intellectual or psychological process but a degeneration, where an underutilized psyche unifies further down than normal circumstances.

Mechanism of Domestication in the Case

1. Perception of the Conscious Gateway:

The sequestered individual elevates the exuberant persona to the status of a "conscious gateway." In this framework, the admired figure becomes a symbolic reservoir or representation of social and psychic vitality.

2. Selective Internalization of General Aspects:

During the domestication process, the individual does not attempt to replicate the entire being of the admired figure (which would require an impossible assimilation of their complete developmental status). Instead, they extract core attributes and integrate them selectively into their own psyche. This allows them to adopt a semblance of social exuberance, thereby reorienting their developmental trajectory toward what they perceive as an ideal state of being.

3. Reconfiguring Identity in Relation to the Other:

With these newly internalized aspects, the individual no longer defines themselves by an independent measure of self-respect. Their identity becomes contingent upon their relationship with the exuberant figure. Their sense of self is now filtered through this external reference point, and their internal dialogue centers on how well they mirror or connect with the idealized persona.

By prioritizing the integration of another's attributes over the cultivation of an autonomous identity, the individual risks subordinating their unique developmental narrative; and, more importantly, their unconscious system. This process diminishes their ability to develop according to personal criteria, as every new encounter is interpreted through the lens of an external ideal.

Fragility of the Social Buffer:

The effectiveness of domestication relies on a robust social buffer. In the absence of sufficient external validation or when the admired persona falls short of expectations, the buffer may collapse. The individual may then experience a profound sense of loss or identity disintegration, reminiscent of the collapse observed during extreme codependency.

Case study: One mentioned in small talk, how the celebrity of yesteryear had an emotional degeneration. The response, as they noted, was: "We do not mention such things." The only result of this identification was such that they domesticated the consciousness of that individual celebrity, so that in their own degeneration, they experienced a personal decay of similar effect.

Simple veneration would not lead to this; only the full, complete investment in the domestication of the celebrity, not as a status, but as the full persona; allowed for the study and encounter of countless mental dynamics, contrasting themselves in relation to it. When they did fail, it was the complete dissolution of their identity; more than the loss of an intimate partner, it was the loss of selfhood, a deep imprint that, even ten years later lingers as an obscurity that cannot be mentioned in small talk.

As the person's sense of self becomes intertwined with the venerated figure, they become vulnerable to fluctuations in that figure's social standing or behavior. A decline in the admired persona's public image could trigger an internal crisis, as the individual's entire self-concept is based on that relationship. Since they rely on the concept rather than the person themselves, the public image is the creation of the concept, meaning they are not only risking the degeneration of the persona itself but also of the public perception that forms the concept.

However, it could be the case that one domesticates their consciousness to the point where it is sophisticated enough; that is, there are enough dynamic interchanges between themselves and their interactions with questions like "What would the persona do in this situation?" In this case, they would not rely on the public concept, as they have built their own. However, when they are dependent on the public image, they are at risk both for the degeneration of the persona itself and for how the public perceives that persona.

Because the public concept is the dependent creator of the composite picture, we can understand that the domestication of consciousness was not fortified in a strong manner. If it had been, they would not need to rely on the public concept. However, the caveat is that public discourse and concepts are considered representations. Even if one recognizes the persona as a representation, they still must adhere in how that representation interacts with the public self-concept, which is also a representation.

V.3 Dramatization, Contest, and the Accessibility of Social Objectives

Contexts of contention arise when there is a general theme to which everyone agrees in their manner of participation, even though no one will receive its full reward. We see this prominently in market exchanges or economically driven systems, where the acquisition or loss of currency becomes the central content of contention; everyone seeks to gain more, and no one wants to lose. Within such contexts, sociality takes shape around the specific roles and behaviors associated with that context of convention; the sociality can proceed to embody specific attributes in the role-playing of that feature.

The dramatization overlay is enabled by a context of contention; there must be competition. A principal award exists that is both universally accessible and yet unattainable without contest. If any participant lacks initial access; particularly in social settings shaped by monetary associations, where someone has no viable means of access; then they are excluded from participation in the social dynamic and its tournament over differentiation or unity. If access is available, yet appears (according to the sociality) uncontested or unlimited, the rest will not engage in that contention; no one fights a battle they cannot win, or that has already been won without struggle.

This dynamic appears consistently in film and theater: a context of contention, or at least resistance, in which there is an objective or end result desired by all characters. Yet, only one can achieve it at any given time. This achievement is never permanent; though it occurs, the contention remains alive. It is a trophy that all can strive for, and one may claim; only to have it contested again. Thus, the sociality maintains its substance through ongoing contention.

If, once the trophy is claimed, it becomes immune to further contest, the social fabric supporting the contention collapses. Likewise, if certain participants can never access the trophy, they disengage from the competition. Or, if the award can be distributed without requiring individual attainment or differentiation, the need for contention disappears.

This pattern is mirrored in economic structures. Currency can exist without generating contention if monetary substantiation is universally accessible. In such a case, few would pursue monetary gain competitively, as the chief objective lacks singularity.

A sociality centered on monetary achievement is only sustainable if all participants have the potential to contend for a singular monetary pinnacle; an achievement that can be both attained and challenged. Without this context of contention, the individual is left without sociality.

Importantly, the purpose of sociality is not the achievement itself but the exchange, the contention around achievement; which correlates with direct access to consciousness, independent of the achievement's symbolic or material encapsulation.

Take, for example, a high school where status becomes the contested field. It is not the status itself that grants direct access to external consciousness, but the arbitrary framework of status-based contention. This structure fosters a setting of social exchange; a medium through which the direct access to consciousness emerges. This consciousness has a materiality not defined by the specific context of contention but instead stands as the encompassing awareness that underlies and transcends its doorstep.

V.4 Domestication, Consciousness, and the Drama of Sociality

Here we arrive at the thesis: developed sociality is essential for purposeful domestication, serving as a remedy for the loss, or obstruction; of direct conscious access. Importantly, this expansion of sociality should not be confused with a mere expansion of relatability. Relatability may offer individuation, but often at the cost of losing contact with consciousness itself.

Take the case of a cult. It may deepen internal relatability among its members but often severs their connection to external consciousness. The cult reaches deep into a form of social intimacy; but this intimacy is not the embodiment of individuation or internalized consciousness. It is the experience of domestication without the weight or consequence of consciousness.

This may seem paradoxical, for domestication in itself is a diminutive version of consciousness, so that without consciousness, we do not have before us a domesticated property. But one can insert a domesticated system; meaning to extract all of consciousness from within their relatability complex; which then can act as a system against the back driver of external consciousness. Every psyche comprises an already domesticated construct so that we can access their relatability to extract formalizations of consciousness. Even without direct access to consciousness, if one asserts a domesticated system, they begin to access the entire spectrum of their latent domesticated encapsulations of consciousness.

This is why all systems begin to access latent infantile domesticated qualities; because they extract from these realms to retain a semblance of consciousness while still asserting a domesticated quality. At this point, it might seem that a cult system would be beneficial, as one begins to gain access to all their domesticated systems. But in fact, what is happening is the actualization of those very latent systems; to which they are latent for a very good reason. Now that they are re-accessed and actualized, these become domineering within the system and cause the forfeiture of any mature development beyond those domesticated elements.

Consequently, if they reach out into the relatability complex of their childhood, they begin to lose mature development through that actualization, becoming individuals who degenerate the entirety of their growth in order to retain that domesticated quality. Naturally, one would reject entering into a domesticated system with no direct access to consciousness. It requires a constant forfeiture of reluctance, so that one begins to lose attainability of all consciousness accessed elsewhere of the domesticated framework being accessed at that moment.

Yet there is one benefit to the cult system: it extracts encapsulations of consciousness through these domesticated constructs, allowing movement beyond those domesticated processes; but at the forfeiture of a mature, standing individual with further developments of consciousness beyond those systems.

What becomes of the later stage in a cult system is an exhaustive domesticated complex of the psyche, which becomes difficult to access, having been exhausted. They no longer have any formalization of consciousness; neither through the preliminary domesticated constructs of their psyche (exhausted) nor by any further consciousness (forfeited initially).

At this point, they begin attempting to access very latent domesticated constructs of their psyche; systems that are infantile or inherited through lineage. They access archetypical ideations impressed upon the psyche, which are improbable for normal social dynamics. Thus, they access rudimentary states of being; the animalistic and illogical constructs of the psyche that lie latent because they do not resemble the expansiveness of the psyche. In the final stage, they enact all these domesticated qualities in an attempt to access any form of consciousness.

This contrasts with expansive sociality, where there is limited direct access to consciousness. This is not about expanding relatability or extracting from previous domesticated complexes of the psyche, but rather pertains directly to the sociality of individuals within that spectrum. At this point, this possibility is not accessible to an individual psyche alone but requires a direct perceptual process of sociality; differing because it requires the perceptual domain more than anything else.

If one is to access the limited direct access of consciousness, it must be through the perceptual realm, and by having the roles within that dynamic of sociality partake at an organizational level embodying individuation, access to consciousness becomes a stronghold despite its limited development. We find this most starkly in institutions, especially educational institutions; where sociality develops through role-playing and the solemn endeavor of that experience. Despite the access being external consciousness, it continues to foster individuation of whatever consciousness it finds, because of the development of that sociality and the contentiousness between fixed roles, differentiation, unity, and the complexities required for a developed state of sociality.

It is, in fact, an experience of the perfected social being in the embodiment of aspects of consciousness; where differentiation, unity, and serious role-playing occur on each side of the equation. Thus, even if the most limited access to consciousness reaches its shores, it will take that substantiation and multiply it two- or three-fold because of the competency of that sociality.

Regular domestication, which lacks complex social effect, individualizes access to consciousness without materializing its details, anchoring itself in a strong sequence relative to that access. Strong access results in strong domestication; weak access results in weak domestication. It reduces itself to infatuation at the point where it can organize without a firm grasp of material form. This is domestication in its most natural state: embodiment at the level of access, absent foundational perspectives.

In complex sociality, although it does not seek to redistribute access or invoke a relatability complex at the expense of consciousness, it does take on the task of processing the finer details of that consciousness at a fundamental level. Each participant fulfills a role infused with infatuation and carries the seriousness of each fragment; not so serious that exchange is halted, but serious enough that contention can be dramatically represented.

This marks the key difference between everyday sociality and its portrayal in theater or film, where the representation is a more intricate embodiment of sociality in relation to access to consciousness. Neither the entertainer nor the audience will accept a diluted version of sociality; it must be dramatized or embodied as a reflection of consciousness and its seriousness, to portray a sociality that the audience can relate to.

It may seem ironic that drama is often seen as distasteful in real life, while in theater or film it is essential for relatability. What distinguishes dramatization in everyday situations, typically viewed negatively, from dramatization in theater or film, where it is valued? Fundamentally, dramatization is positive because it communicates the seriousness of sociality to a degree that allows participants to engage in an exchange where, both in performance and reception, a third-party perspective becomes accessible. In actual sociality, this can be experienced as a conscious sentiment, regardless of the level of access.

Another common feature in film and theater is the frequent starting point of limited access to consciousness, which then necessitates complex sociality to generate relatability for the audience. If consciousness were more directly accessed, dramatization and social complexity might seem excessive. There would be no need for such structures when consciousness is fully transparent. Thus, most films and plays begin with limited access to consciousness as a necessary condition to justify dramatization.

In real-life sociality, dramatization is often perceived negatively, especially when the embodiment of an encapsulation of consciousness cannot be exchanged through roles. But where there is sufficient exchange, dramatization should be seen in a positive light; it becomes an expression of complex sociality. The negative perception often arises because dramatization in real life is not seen through the lens of developmental experience or with the third-party view an audience brings to theater. Yet this third-party view is essential to complex sociality: it allows us to engage purposefully with consciousness without mistaking seriousness for absolute reality.

This conflict underlies the disillusionment with complex sociality, where seriousness can seem detached from the broader reality; as if the dramatization exceeds the context it is meant to serve. It is the overextension of dramatization that leads to this breakdown, leaving little room for mutual recognition or exchange. We are all participants in potential exchange; the seriousness of one role should allow others to emerge and remain capable of engaging. Ideally, full exchange, or permeability between exchanges; would transcend dramatization entirely, allowing everyone to engage in each other's movements. In such a society, dramatization would not be necessary.

All participants must maintain a third-party perspective, akin to an audience watching a performance. This audience-consciousness must persist throughout the exchange, whether someone is actively dramatizing or receiving that dramatization; so that everyone receives the experience itself, rather than defaulting to either full validation of the dramatizing role or disillusionment of the recipient role. In this way, complex sociality serves the broader objective of consciousness rather than merely reinforcing itself.

The very possibility of contention, or dramatization; emerges when sociality presents itself through roles ready for exchange in accordance with a specific context of contention.